AS/A-LEVEL
Economics

John Hearn

ESSENTIAL WORD
DICTIONARY

To my mother and sister for being who they are,
my father for being who he was, and my sons
Ben and Chris for their inspiration.

Philip Allan Updates
Market Place
Deddington
Oxfordshire
OX15 0SE

Tel: 01869 338652
Fax: 01869 337590
e-mail: sales@philipallan.co.uk
www.philipallan.co.uk

ISBN 0 86003 370 8

Acknowledgements
My thanks to Dr Peter Smith for his comments, Dr Edmund Cannon for
his help, and special thanks to my wife, Geraldine, not only for the word-
processing but also for her critical eye that added value to this dictionary.

Printed by Raithby, Lawrence & Co Ltd, Leicester

Introduction

This is a concise dictionary of words used in A-level economics, where the brevity comes not from the explanation of each entry but through the care with which each word has been chosen for inclusion.

It is important to realise that many words in economics have a slightly different meaning to those accepted by the layperson. For example, *The Concise Oxford Dictionary* defines scarcity as 'seldom meet with, rare, hard to find'. In economics anything that requires an allocative mechanism is scarce, although neither a loaf of bread nor an apple could be described as rare or hard to find. Definitions vary even across the social sciences. For example, business studies defines profit as 'a surplus left over after the costs of land, labour and capital have been deducted' and the Inland Revenue agrees with this definition for tax purposes. However, the economist considers part of the surplus to be a cost of enterprise and says that true profit is any surplus over and above the minimum required to keep the entrepreneur in that line of business.

In this dictionary, each word is broken down into a maximum of four parts or a minimum of one. Each entry begins with a single sentence definition. A second paragraph often expands and further explains the word. Where relevant, there is then an example which may be a table or a graph. Lastly, there is sometimes a tip where a word is commonly misunderstood, confused with another word, used in error or found in conjunction with other words in the dictionary. There may also be a reference to a word's contextual relevance or its relative importance as, even in an essential words dictionary, some entries are more important than others. Throughout the dictionary there are italicised cross-references to other words that you may need to refer to in order to fully understand an entry.

If you are completing the A-level in economics, it is essential you recognise and understand all the terms in this dictionary. Many of the words are relevant to AS, while some are specific to the modules in A2. To help you identify these, a list of the most important terms for each part of the AS and A-level specifications for AQA, Edexcel and OCR is included in an appendix (see page 155).

abnormal profit: when the profit of a firm is above or below *normal profit*.

▨ When profit is above normal, abnormal profit is described as supernormal profit or *excessive profit*; below normal profit is described as *subnormal profit*.

▨ *TIP* A common error is to assume that abnormal and supernormal are synonymous and to forget that anything less than normal is also abnormal.

absolute advantage: when one productive unit, such as a firm, can use the same number of inputs to produce more output than another productive unit.

▨ Absolute advantage is sometimes referred to as an 'absolute cost advantage' when the same product is produced at a lower unit cost. The term is used in an explanation of the advantages of specialisation both for internal trade and for international trade. See *comparative advantage*.

absolute price: this is nothing more than the magnitude of a number which, in terms of a product, is measured in units of money.

▨ *TIP* It is important to recognise the difference between absolute and *relative price*.

accelerator theory: a theory of how a change in national income affects investment.

▨ In its simplest form, the accelerator theory can be expressed as $I = f(\Delta Y)$, i.e. investment is a function of a change in national income. The theory also assumes a fixed capital:output ratio.

▨ *e.g.* Assume there are 1,000 units of capital in the economy of which 100 (or 10%) are replaced each year. Suppose national output doubles, then in order to maintain the fixed capital:output ratio during the first year, investment in capital will rise from 100 to 1,100 units, causing a further acceleration in output before settling back at 200 replacement units per year or 10% of 2,000.

▨ *TIP* The accelerator theory is part of the Keynesian analysis of economic instability and is usually analysed alongside the *multiplier* effect of autonomous investment on national income. Do not confuse the two: the accelerator is the induced effect on investment of a change in national income; the multiplier is the effect of an autonomous change in investment on national income.

accommodating monetary policy: in Keynesian economics, the management of aggregate demand requires a *monetary policy* that accommodates or reacts to the real changes taking place or planned for the economy.

a

■ *TIP* Keynesians argue that *inflation* requires an accommodating growth in the money supply, while monetarists argue that excessive growth in the money supply is the cause of inflation.

active money balance: money which is flowing through the economy as opposed to an idle money balance which is withdrawn from the flow of income.

■ In Keynesian *liquidity preference theory*, active balances include money held for transactions and precautionary motives, while the speculative motive is an idle balance.

■ *TIP* There is some debate about whether the precautionary demand for money is an idle balance rather than an active balance as it is unlikely to be used for long periods of time.

adaptive expectations: expectations which adjust as current and forecasted events change.

■ These changes in expectations can have a real impact on the economy.

■ *e.g.* The adaptive expectation theory of inflation suggests that the expectation of a rise in inflation raises wage demands and may cause a wage-price spiral.

administered price: when prices are established by a conscious decision rather than by the interaction of supply and demand.

■ *e.g.* The government may fix the exchange rate or interest rate in pursuit of a policy rather than as a response to market forces. Administered prices also include price-fixing by oligopolists and monopolists.

ad valorem tax: an expenditure tax which is added to the price of a product.

■ This tax is a percentage of the value of a product whereas other expenditure taxes can be a specific amount, such as 1p on a pint of beer or 5p on a litre of petrol.

■ *e.g.* Value added tax (VAT).

advertising: the use of mass media to promote a product in order to stimulate demand and increase sales.

■ Substantial increases in sales can be obtained through creating brand image, brand loyalty and product differentiation. Advertising is often categorised as being either informative or persuasive.

■ *TIP* At one extreme, advertising is viewed as a waste of time and money that brings about an inefficient allocation of resources. At the other extreme, it is considered an essential cost that creates the market in which a firm can expand and take full advantage of economies of scale.

aggregate demand (also called 'aggregate expenditure'): the total nominal demand or expenditure on products by consumers, governments, foreigners and producers within an economy over a specified time period.

aggregate demand curve: the functional relationship between the average level of prices in an economy and the total quantity of products demanded (see diagram below).

■ *TIP* When the aggregate demand curve is combined with the aggregate supply curve, it can be used as a simple equilibrium model for an economy.

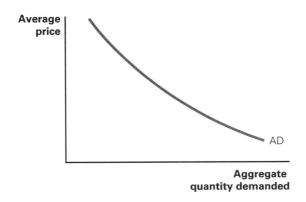

aggregate demand shock: a sudden and unexpected change in any of the components of aggregate demand.
- Shocks may have important real effects on the economy, such as a significant change in the level of employment, or they may have only nominal effects, such as mild inflation. All these shocks cause the demand curve to shift.

aggregate expenditure: see *aggregate demand*.

aggregate supply: the total output of domestic industry, including consumer products and capital goods, over a specific time period.
- *TIP* In the short term, aggregate supply is thought to be affected by changes in aggregate demand. In the longer term, it is the factors which promote economic growth that are significant in increasing supply.

aggregate supply curve: a curve which shows the functional relationship between changes in the output of an economy and changes in the average price level.
- These curves are now popularly used in general equilibrium models and come in a variety of shapes, depending on the theoretical assumptions underpinning them, as shown below.

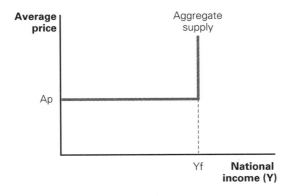

Extreme Keynesians assume that price remains stable at Ap until *full employment* is achieved at Yf, at which point the supply curve becomes vertical.

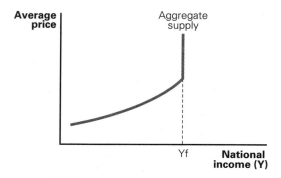

Less extreme Keynesians accept that a rising average level of prices may expand output up to full employment Yf, after which the curve becomes vertical.

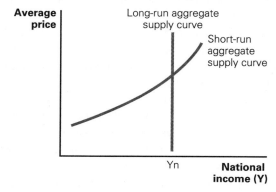

Other economists accept fluctuations in output with changes in the average price level in the short run, but argue for a long-run vertical aggregate supply function at the natural level of employment, Yn.

aggregate supply shock: a change which occurs as a result of unexpected events that shift the aggregate supply curve.

■ *e.g.* Shocks are caused by natural disasters, such as floods, famines and storms; human disasters, such as wars; and economic events, such as sudden changes in oil prices and technology.

allocative efficiency: when there is an optimum (best) allocation of resources between consumers and producers.

■ This is said to occur when firms are producing under *perfect competition* so that the price of the product is equal to the marginal cost of producing it. The price reflects the consumers' valuation of the usefulness of the product, while the marginal cost reflects the additional cost to society of allocating resources to its production. It would be allocatively inefficient if the price consumers were willing to pay was less or more than the additional cost to society of the resources used up in the production process.

■ *TIP* The recognition of an *externality* at the level of either production or consumption can create allocative inefficiency.

allocative mechanism: the way in which scarce resources are allocated between users.

▦ At one extreme, a free market allocates resources through the price mechanism, while at the other extreme a command economy allocates resources through a central authority. Between the two extremes, a mixture of commands and prices are involved in the allocative mechanism.

▦ *TIP* In reality, all economies are a mixture of commands and prices tending towards one or other of the theoretical extremes.

anticipated inflation: the expected future rate of increase in the average level of prices.

▦ *TIP* Anticipated inflation plays an important part in framing government economic policy as well as influencing wage negotiations. It is, however, dependent upon the forecasting source and which theory is used to explain the cause of inflation.

anti–competitive practice: action taken by firms or other economic agents to reduce the level of competition in a market.

▦ It is a point of argument whether such practice may be considered beneficial to an economy when, say, a government issues a patent that gives exclusive rights to one firm to produce a product; or whether or not the efficient allocation of resources is damaged by firms which act to reduce competition in order to restrict consumer choice and boost profits.

anti–trust: American terminology for legislation that controls the development of *monopoly*, dominant firm and various restrictive practices.

▦ The policy which controls this legislation is described as non-discretionary so that it is illegal to contravene the laws irrespective of whether or not it may be in the national interest to allow certain restrictive practices to proceed.

▦ *TIP* In the UK, monopoly policy adopts a discretionary approach which allows greater flexibility of interpretation than in the US.

appreciation: usually refers to a rise in the price of one currency measured in terms of another currency.

▦ This means the same quantity of the appreciated currency buys more of the foreign currency. Alternatively, appreciation is used to describe an increase in the value of any asset.

▦ *TIP* The term appreciation is used when the exchange rate rises in a floating system. In a *fixed exchange rate* system it is usual to refer to a *revaluation* when a currency is raised to a new fixed level. A fall in the price of a currency or asset is termed *depreciation*.

arbitrage: trading the same product between two or more markets to take advantage of a price difference.

▦ A profit can be made by simultaneously buying the item in one market and selling it in the other market. Arbitrage often takes place in foreign exchange markets where different time zones and lags in the rate at which information is transferred can create profitable opportunities.

■ *TIP* Arbitrage should not be confused with *speculation*. Unlike arbitrage, which requires the observation of different prices at the same point in time, speculation requires the passage of time, i.e. a person buys an item in anticipation that its price will rise in the future.

arbitration: where an impartial third party is asked to help settle a dispute.

■ Arbitration is commonly associated with labour market disputes, particularly in wage claims. See *pendulum arbitration*.

arc elasticity: see *price elasticity of demand*.

asset: an item which is owned by an individual or group and has exchange value.

■ An individual's wealth is made up of the sum of the value of his or her assets. Assets are often divided into tangible physical assets, such as buildings and machinery, and intangible financial assets, such as money, deposit accounts, stocks and shares.

at factor cost: usually a national income measure which excludes indirect taxes but includes subsidies.

■ As UK national accounting moves into line with European standards, so this measure is being phased out.

at market price: usually a national income measure which includes indirect taxes but excludes subsidies.

augmented Phillips curve: incorporates a price variable into the original Phillips curve. See *Phillips curve*.

■ The predictive ability of the original curve was brought into question in the 1970s when inflation and unemployment rose together and a revised version of the Phillips curve, the augmented Phillips curve or the expectations-adjusted Phillips curve, was introduced.

■ *e.g.* Essentially, the augmented Phillips curve is a short-run phenomenon which moves around a stable long-run *non-accelerating inflation rate of unemployment* (NAIRU). The NAIRU is a vertical line above the natural rate of unemployment which is represented by U in the diagram below. Any

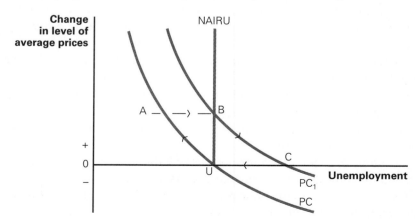

short-term movement from, say, U to A along PC caused by an unanticipated change in inflationary demand moves back to B in the long term, while a slowing of inflationary demand moves down a new short-run Phillips curve PC_1 to C and returns to U in the long run.

automatic stabiliser: a reaction to changes in the economy that suppresses the direction of fluctuations in economic activity.

▓ Keynesian analysis maintains that the automatic stabiliser reduces the amplitude of cyclical events.

▓ *e.g.* In an expanding economy, tax from increasing income acts as a stabiliser. Alternatively, in a contracting economy, unemployment benefits and welfare payments act to reverse the decline.

autonomous expenditure: spending which occurs independently of any changes in the level of national income.

autonomous investment: investment in capital which is unrelated to changes in the level of national income.

▓ *TIP* Economic analysis differentiates autonomous investment which changes income from that of *induced investment* which is changed by income.

average cost: the total cost (C) of using all factor inputs divided by the number of units produced (Q), expressed as AC = TC/Q.

▓ Diagrammatically, an average cost function is normally assumed to be U-shaped as illustrated below.

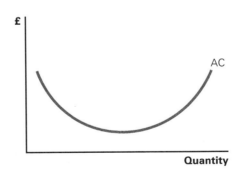

The shape results from economic variables that are likely to reduce average costs as output starts to increase, but will eventually raise average costs past a certain point.

average cost pricing: when firms set a price for their products based upon the average cost of production plus an agreed mark-up or profit.

▓ *TIP* This type of pricing policy is often described as an alternative to a profit-maximising pricing policy.

average fixed cost: the total fixed cost (TFC) of production divided by the number of units produced (Q), expressed as AFC = TFC/Q.

▓ The normal shape for an average fixed cost function is a curve that falls towards, but never reaches, the horizontal axis as output expands (see overleaf).

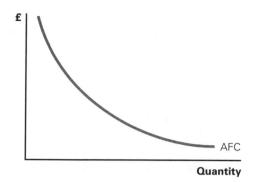

■ TIP Since fixed costs remain the same at all levels of output including zero, the average fixed cost always falls towards zero. Mathematicians refer to this situation as a number that reaches zero at infinity.

average product: the total product (TP) or output of a productive unit divided by the number of factor inputs (FI) required to achieve that level of production, expressed as AP = TP/FI.

average propensity to consume: the proportion of income (Y) that is spent (C) on goods and services, expressed as APC = C/Y.

average propensity to import: the proportion of income (Y) that is spent on foreign products (M), expressed as APM = M/Y.

average propensity to pay tax: the proportion of income (Y) that is paid to government in the form of tax (T), expressed as APT = T/Y.

average propensity to save: the proportion of income (Y) that is not spent or is saved (S), expressed as APS = S/Y.

average revenue: the total revenue (TR) received from the sale of a product divided by the number of units of that product sold (Q), expressed as AR = TR/Q.

average revenue product: the total revenue received from the sale of a product (TRP) divided by the number of factor inputs (FI) required to achieve that level of production and sales, expressed as ARP = TRP/FI.

■ TIP Students often muddle AR and ARP. Remember that to derive AR, divide by the number of units of output, while to derive ARP, divide by the number of factor inputs used to produce that output.

average variable cost: the total variable cost (TVC) of production divided by the number of units produced (Q), expressed as AVC = TVC/Q.

■ Of the two components that make up average total cost, namely average variable cost and average fixed cost, average variable cost is likely to fall as output begins to expand, but eventually rises to give the average cost curve its normal U-shape.

backward bending supply curve of labour: illustrates that the functional relationship between the wage rate and the individual supply of effort or number of hours worked per day rises positively up to a point where it bends backwards or becomes negative.

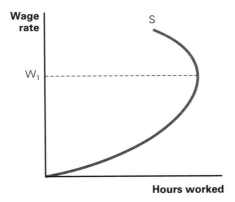

- As the wage rate rises to W_1, the individual worker is attracted to work more hours and give up leisure time. However, at some wage rate/hours worked, leisure time becomes more valuable and a rise in the wage rate means that the same level of income can be maintained working fewer hours.
- *TIP* Do not confuse this curve with that for the supply of labour to a particular market or occupation. That curve is positively sloped and shows the relationship between the wage rate and the number of people who are willing to work in that labour market. It does not show the number of hours each person is willing to work.

backward integration: see *vertical integration*.

balanced budget: in the government budget, the current revenue received from taxation over a given time (usually 1 year) is equal to the current expenditure by government over that same period.

balanced budget multiplier: always has a value of 1 such that a rise of, say, £10 million in both government expenditure (an injection into the flow of income) and taxation (a withdrawal from the flow) will raise national income by £10 million.

■ *e.g.* Suppose the *marginal propensity* to consume was 0.75 and the marginal propensity to withdraw (MPW) was 0.25. Using the formula K = 1/MPW (see *multiplier*), the value of the multiplier = 1/0.25 = 4. Therefore, an injection of £10 million would raise national income by £10 × 4 = £40 million. The withdrawal from the circular flow would be (MPC × £10 million) × 4 = (0.75 × £10 million) × 4 = £30 million. National income would therefore have risen by £10 million.

■ *TIP* Whichever numbers are substituted for MPC and MPW, the result is always 1 × the change, as long as the budget is moving from one zero balance to another. Students often mistakenly believe that the taxation withdrawal cancels out the expenditure injection, so be careful not to answer 'no change in national income'.

balance of invisibles: the difference, on the balance of payments, between the value of exports and imports in the form of services such as banking, insurance and tourism, over a given time period.

balance of payments: the difference between the total payments into and out of a country, measured in domestic currency, over a given period of time.

■ Overall it always has a value of zero and therefore academic interest is focused on its many subdivisions which do not produce a zero balance. It is usual to start by looking at the balance on current account and to state that the balance on capital account will be equal and opposite. However, it is clearer to recognise that the capital account has two parts: financial flows that have no official direction; and official financing of the deficit or surplus that results from the sum of all flows on current and unofficial capital account.

■ *e.g.* A simplified balance of payments is shown below.

Balance of trade	−250	
Invisible balance	+150	
Current balance		−100
Balance of transactions in UK		
(assets and liabilities)	−75	
Balancing item	+25	
Capital balance		−50
Total currency flow		−150
Total official financing		+150

■ *TIP* It is important to distinguish between balances and totals. Note that all the statistics in the example above are numbers which represent the differences between two totals — they do not reveal how small or large the totals are.

balance of payments disequilibrium: a fundamental imbalance between the current and/or capital flows (excluding official financing) which leads to a persistent reduction or increase in long-term foreign currency loans and/or foreign exchange reserves.

▨ *TIP* A disequilibrium can be a surplus or a deficit, although the history of the UK balance of payments has often led to a disequilibrium being mistakenly interpreted as a deficit only. Remember that the overall balance of payments, including official financing, has a zero balance. The disequilibrium therefore refers to an imbalance within the accounts.

balance of payments equilibrium: occurs over a period of time when there is no tendency to increase or decrease long-term foreign currency loans and/or foreign exchange reserves.

▨ *TIP* It is statistically improbable that any single month's balance of payments account will produce a zero balance (excluding official financing). There is usually a temporary surplus or deficit. Over time, however, these cancel each other out if the accounts are in equilibrium.

balance of trade (also called 'visible balance')**:** the difference between the value of imported and exported goods over a specified period of time.

▨ This account on the balance of payments is sometimes referred to as the visible balance because it deals only in tangible goods, whereas services are accounted for on the *invisible balance*.

▨ *TIP* There is a tendency in the popular press to imply that deficits or surpluses on the balance of trade are important to the wellbeing of an economy. This is not strictly correct, as the balance on current account is the most significant balance. In the UK economy, a deficit on the visible balance of trade is usually offset, or partially offset, by a surplus on the invisible account. When the visible and invisible accounts are put together as the current account, it is easier to identify good or bad news.

balance sheet: an accounting term which offsets the value of all the assets of a firm against the value of all its liabilities on a specified date.

▨ *TIP* It is important to recognise that the balance sheet of a bank enters the same number twice so that it appears on each side of the account. This is because although a deposit is a liability to the bank while it is owned by the customer, it is also an asset that the bank can use to derive an income as long as it remains on deposit.

balances with the Bank of England: cash held on behalf of the *commercial banks*.

▨ At the end of the trading day, interbank indebtedness has to be settled by a transfer of cash between accounts held at the Bank of England. Commercial banks use these accounts in the same way that their customers use current accounts to settle debts.

balancing item: the amount which appears in the published accounts of the *balance of payments*, representing an estimate of the sum of errors and omissions and having a value that equalises what has been paid for with what has been imported.

bank: a financial intermediary authorised by the *Bank of England* to accept deposits from and make loans to its customers.

▨ There are a variety of banks, ranging from merchant banks, which deal mainly with business customers, to commercial or retail banks, which deal with individuals.

bank credit: money created when a bank expands a customer's spending power by adding a loan (advance) to his or her current account.

▨ The earliest banks only undertook the safe-keeping of assets, usually gold. Once these institutions realised that they had an opportunity to increase their earnings by making loans, a major component of modern money was created.

bank credit multiplier (also known as 'money multiplier'): the number of times the assets of a bank can change as a result of a change in its cash or reserve base.

▨ The formula used to make this calculation is usually expressed as:

$$\text{BCM} = \frac{100\%}{\text{required reserve or cash base}}$$

▨ *e.g.* If the required reserve or cash base is 10%, the BCM = 100%/10% = 10%. If it is 20%, the BCM = 100%/20% = 5%. The BCM illustrates how, in pursuit of monetary policy, the *Bank of England* can have a significant influence on aggregate monetary demand by making relatively small adjustments to the reserve or cash base of commercial banks.

▨ *TIP* Remember the change in the reserve base is always included in the total effect of a multiplier calculation. Suppose the multiplier is 5 and there is an increase of £100 in the reserve base with no cash drain to the public. The result is a rise in bank assets and liabilities of £500 (£400 from new activity and £100 from the original change).

bank note: originally a receipt for the deposit of gold with goldsmiths, hence the phrase 'I promise to pay the bearer on demand the sum of ...' which still appears on bank notes. Now, however, the promise is not honoured in gold. Presentation of a £20 note to the *Bank of England* merely results in receipt of another £20 note in its place.

Bank of England: the UK's central bank.

▨ The Bank of England was set up in 1694 under William III, and granted special privileges in return for a loan of £1.2 million. Its structure was established under the 1844 Bank Charter Act which separated its role as a bank from that of an issuer of notes. It remained a private bank until 1946 when it was nationalised. Following this, the Bank of England played a subordinate role under the guidance of the *Treasury*. In 1997, the Labour government gave it greater independence and charged it with the responsibility of achieving a prescribed inflation target.

▨ *TIP* The role of the Bank of England in the overall management of the economy is not clearly understood by economists and different opinions are voiced by various schools of thought. Opposing views are held by the monetarists and the Keynesians.

bank rate: the rate at which the *Bank of England* is prepared to lend to commercial banks.

▨ It is now far less important than when it was officially announced as the minimum rate at which the Bank of England would rediscount first class bills. Between 1971 and 1981 the bank rate was renamed the *minimum lending rate* (MLR) and recognised as the cornerstone of government monetary policy. Today, an announcement of bank rate (base rate) changes by the *Monetary Policy Committee* (MPC) is still interpreted as a signal of the direction of *monetary policy*.

bankruptcy: the legal procedure that takes place when a company becomes insolvent.

▨ The control of the company is transferred to the official receiver and a trustee is appointed to realise any assets and distribute them to creditors and then, if anything remains, to the owners.

barriers to entry: invisible obstacles that make it difficult or impossible for new firms to enter an industry.

▨ The theories of *monopoly* and *oligopoly* involve entry barriers which may include natural barriers such as the uneven distribution of natural resources, or technical barriers which result from economies of scale and transport cost advantages. Also, there may be deliberate barriers created by patents, tariffs, quotas and other anti-competitive practices.

barter: the direct exchange of one product for another without the use of a monetary medium.

▨ In primitive societies, barter preceded the use of money. Today, it may take place between countries where one or both of their currencies are not freely convertible.

▨ *TIP* Reference to barter in examinations usually concentrates on its disadvantages, i.e. it requires a double coincidence of wants, it has no standard unit of account and products may be indivisible and difficult to store.

base rate: a rate of interest that commercial banks charge on a risk-free loan.

▨ As there is always an element of risk, customers pay an interest rate which is comprised of the base rate plus a number of percentage points which are an assessment of that risk. When the term is related to the *Bank of England*, it is an informed reference to the *bank rate*.

bear market: where asset values, usually shares, are falling on average over a significant period of time.

▨ In this type of market, a person who sells assets in anticipation of buying them back at a lower price in the future is referred to as a bear. The opposite situation is referred to as a *bull market*.

bill discounting: when a commercial bill or government bill is purchased at a rate less than its face value.

bill of exchange: a financial security that includes a promise to pay the holder of the bill a specified sum of money on a specified future date.

▨ Because bills of exchange usually mature within a few months, they are considered relatively liquid assets when discounted. Commercial banks are significant buyers of these assets which can be held in their reserve base.

b

black economy: that part of the economy where trade is not recorded and therefore does not register in national income statistics.

■ Activity in the black economy may or may not be illegal.

■ *e.g.* It is illegal to sell certain drugs at present and it was illegal to sell alcohol in the United States during prohibition. However, it is not illegal to mow a neighbour's lawn for pocket money, although the activity is unlikely to be recorded in official statistics and is therefore part of the black economy.

■ *TIP* As a rule of thumb, the more a government intervenes in an economy, the greater the size of the black economy.

black market: an unofficial or secondary market which exists because a price has been fixed below the market clearing price in a primary market, and a supply of the product is available for resale.

■ *e.g.* Secondary markets often exist for the tickets at cup finals, rock concerts and international rugby matches. Government rationing can also lead to an illegal black market.

blue chip: the name given to the shares of highly rated companies which have a very low risk of default.

bond: a financial security issued by a company or the government as a form of long-term loan.

■ Bonds are usually issued for 1 or more years and pay a nominal rate of interest. The capital value of the bond can vary over the term of its life, but will be repaid in full at maturity.

■ *TIP* Bonds are significant in the Keynesian explanation of the *speculative demand for money*. When interest rates are thought to be at their lowest and the next move is expected to be a rise, bond prices will fall, and the speculator will hold money before buying the bonds at a lower price in the future.

branding: the creation of an image for a product which differentiates it from similar products in the marketplace.

■ Successful branding of a product can shift the demand curve to the right as well as make demand less responsive to price rises, i.e. more price inelastic.

■ *TIP* Branding is an important component in the theories of imperfect competition. Successful branding usually requires significant expenditure on advertising.

brand loyalty: when customers who are satisfied with a product tend to ignore competitive products in the advice they give to other people and repeat-purchase the product themselves.

■ Brand loyalty has a significant effect on the price elasticity of demand, i.e. the greater the brand loyalty, the less sensitivity to a price change.

brand name: the focal point for the image created by *branding*.

■ It helps the process of separation between similar products and, once registered in the UK, cannot be used by other companies.

■ *e.g.* Some brand names have been adopted as the generic term for an item, e.g. vacuum cleaners are often referred to using the brand name Hoover. Other strong brand names include Disney, Cadbury's, Kellogg's, Sony, Levi's and Mercedes Benz.

brand proliferation: when large firms in *oligopolistic* markets create apparent competition by slight changes in their products and a new image leading to many seemingly competitive products all owned by the same company.

■ *e.g.* Many washing powders, which are apparently competing with each other, are owned by Procter & Gamble or Unilever.

Bretton Woods: a location in New Hampshire, USA, where in 1944 an international conference agreed to set up the *International Monetary Fund*, the *International Bank for Reconstruction and Development* (World Bank) and a system of *convertible currencies* based on *fixed exchange rates*.

■ *TIP* In terms of economic history, this ground-breaking conference set the scene for a significant period (1947–71) of stability and growth in world trade.

budget: a statement of future plans to spend money and finance that expenditure.

■ Although reference to a budget is made at the level of analysis of the firm and the consumer, the most common use is when referring to the government budget. This annual statement by the government is a plan of its expenditure and revenue raising for the forthcoming fiscal year.

■ *TIP* The government's budget is not only analysed at the level of *taxation* and expenditure. It can also indicate the type of policy that government is using to manage the overall level of economic activity. In this situation, it is referred to as budgetary or *fiscal policy* and forms an important part of Keynesian theory.

budget deficit: the excess of government expenditure over taxation.

■ In crude terms, it is often referred to as the *public sector borrowing requirement* (PSBR), although strictly this also includes the debts of local government and the remaining nationalised industries. According to *Keynes*, when an economy is settled at a level of less than full employment, the government should budget for a deficit and expand the aggregate demand for goods and services.

budget line: in consumer theory this shows the various combinations of two products that can be purchased at given prices and income.

■ The budget line is also commonly known as the consumption possibility line and its slope is determined by the price ratio of the two products. The line is also a boundary between what can and cannot be afforded.

budget surplus: the excess of taxation over government expenditure.

■ A budget surplus can be used to make a *public sector debt repayment* (PSDR), although this depends on the fiscal policies being pursued. *Keynes* argued that when an economy is overheating at a level of over full employment, the government should reduce aggregate demand by budgeting for a surplus.

buffer stock: a reserve of a commodity held to stabilise commodity prices.

■ The stocks are held by a third party, usually government. When a surplus is produced, in order to maintain a given price or price range, the product is purchased and added to the buffer stock. Alternatively, a shortage leads to stocks being run down as they are sold in order to maintain price.

■ *e.g.* Agricultural produce and metals.

■ *TIP* This policy for stabilising prices has only met with limited success in the past and is often criticised because the level of knowledge required to manage the system efficiently is not available. The term is also used to describe the minimum stock a firm holds as a buffer against unforeseen events.

bull market: where asset values, usually shares, are on average rising over a significant period of time.

■ In this type of market, a person who buys assets in anticipation of selling them at a higher price in the future is referred to as a bull. The opposite situation is referred to as a *bear market*.

call money: lent to the discount houses by banks at a relatively low rate of interest on the proviso that, if required, it can be returned to them in cash within 24 hours. See *discount market*.

For the commercial banks, this asset is the next most liquid after *till money* and balances held at the *Bank of England*. It allows UK banks to hold much lower cash reserves than many foreign banks.

Cambridge school: Cambridge University is distinguished by an influential school of economics and economists starting with *Alfred Marshall* and including Arthur Cecil Pigou (see *Pigovian tax*), *John Maynard Keynes*, Joan Robinson, Nicholas Kaldor and Piero Staffa.

Although there is not one general view, there is a loose alliance among these economists who prefer their economic models to include historical, sociological and psychological factors. The modern Cambridge School has been closely associated with Keynesian and neo-Keynesian economics.

TIP Although not essential, it can be helpful in examinations to recognise, where relevant, those economists who have had a significant effect on the development of economic thinking.

canons of taxation: four principles which were laid down by *Adam Smith* and are still broadly adhered to.

Smith's principles are: equity, in that the burden of tax matches people's ability to pay; certainty, in terms of information about tax being transparent; convenience of payment and collection; and economy in the cost of administration and collection.

CAP: see *Common Agricultural Policy*.

capacity output: the level of a firm's output which produces the lowest average cost of production in the long run.

capital: one of the *factors of production* that is distinguished from the other factors because it is a produced means of production.

e.g. Machinery.

capital consumption: a value for the capital used up in the production process.

e.g. In the process of production, a machine undergoes wear and tear and requires maintenance until it is finally replaced. In the national accounts, a value for capital consumption is used to distinguish between how much investment in capital is required to maintain productive capacity and how much new capital has been added to productive capacity.

capital deepening: an increase in the amount of capital available to each unit of labour.

■ It is usually a prerequisite of economic growth that there is capital deepening.

capital gains tax: a tax levied in the UK on any realised gains in the value of assets specified by the Inland Revenue.

■ Capital gains can accrue without a tax liability until they are realised through a sale. In the past, capital gains tax was levied on increases in nominal value irrespective of any real gains. More recently, there has been an attempt to adjust value for *inflation* through the indexation of acquisition costs.

capital intensity: the ratio of capital to labour used in the production process.

■ In one direction the production process is described as being capital intensive, while in the other it is described as being labour intensive.

■ *e.g.* Many of the industries in less developed countries are described as *labour intensive*, while the industries of more developed countries are capital intensive.

capitalism: an economic system for allocating scarce resources that requires property rights to be predominantly private and the price mechanism to signal changes in each of many marketplaces.

■ Government intervention is restricted to where markets fail to allocate resources efficiently. There is, however, a significant level of debate among economists about the amount of intervention required to compensate for *market failure*.

capital:labour ratio: the rate at which units of capital and labour are combined in the productive process.

capital market: a market which is divided into a primary market concerned with the issue of new securities, and a secondary market where second-hand dealing in these securities can take place.

■ The advantage to a firm of issuing new shares is that it avoids a commitment to pay regular interest payments and the final repayment which takes place with a loan. This can be particularly useful to a firm in the early stages of development. The primary market includes *issuing houses* and *underwriters*, while the main institution of the secondary market is the *stock exchange* with a few minor exchanges such as EASDAQ and Techmark.

■ *TIP* It is a common error to refer to the stock exchange as the institution that deals in new issues. In fact, the stock exchange only deals in second-hand securities.

capital transfer tax: a tax on the value of assets transferred from one person to another or others either in the form of gifts or as the result of an inheritance.

■ *TIP* Do not confuse these taxes, which require the person receiving the transfer to pay the tax, with a capital gains tax, where the person who sells an asset may become liable to the tax.

C

capital widening: when an increase in units of labour is matched by an increase in capital that maintains the same capital:labour ratio.

■ *TIP* Do not confuse this with *capital deepening* which increases the capital:labour ratio.

cartel: a group of firms which agree restrictive practices, usually by fixing price or output.

■ Such practices may be investigated as anti-competitive and are designed to benefit the producers and disadvantage the consumer.

cash: the bank notes and coins issued as *legal tender* by the officially recognised monetary authority.

■ *TIP* It is a common mistake to confuse *money* and cash. All cash is money but not all money is cash. *Cheques* and *credit cards* can be used as money but, although they are claims on cash, they are not cash. An interesting point is that if all these claims on cash were exercised simultaneously, then only a small fraction could be honoured immediately.

cash ratio: the ratio of cash to money that exists in the monetary system.

■ This concept is important to financial institutions such as banks where sufficient cash reserves must be maintained by the bank to satisfy both everyday demand for cash and unforeseen heavy demand. A look at the asset structure of a bank shows how this is done. The cash ratio held by banks may be imposed on them by a central bank or may be enshrined in the rules of 'sound banking practice', i.e. the rules that maintain customer confidence. Past banking collapses have resulted from demands for cash that could not be met from liquid assets.

central bank: the institution within a country that acts as a banker to government, a lender of last resort to other banks, and an instrument of monetary policy.

■ Around the world, central banks have varying degrees of independence where some act in pursuance of defined targets without reference to their governments, while others act only under the direction of their governments.

■ *e.g.* Bank of England, Federal Reserve (USA), Bundesbank (Germany).

centrally planned economy (also called 'command economy'): in such an economy, the means of production are state controlled and the allocation of resources is managed centrally.

■ Gradually, centrally planned economies such as those in Eastern Europe, are making way for free markets and private property rights. Some countries, e.g. China, have moved towards a command capitalism in which there is economic freedom, but no political freedom.

■ *TIP* Essay questions commonly compare free market and command economies. Those which ask about the changeover from one to the other require students to consider transition costs. See *transitional economy*.

certificate of deposit: a savings contract between a depositor and a *bank* that is for a fixed term of between 3 months and 5 years, paying a higher rate of interest than other savings accounts.

■ Because contracts are for fixed terms, there is a lively second-hand market where these assets can be bought and sold at a discount.

ceteris paribus: Latin for 'other things being equal'.

■ To simplify the complexities of economic analysis, it is often necessary to isolate one or two variables and analyse the impact of a change assuming other things do not change.

■ *e.g.* In order to analyse the relationship between price and quantity demanded, it is necessary to assume that a price change is not accompanied by any change in the other factors which can affect demand.

■ *TIP* A critical evaluation of theory needs to recognise that in the real world many things are likely to change at the same time.

Chancellor of the Exchequer: the political mouthpiece of the *Treasury* who is responsible for the annual budget in particular and fiscal policy in general.

cheque: a written instruction to a *bank* on official paper to pay the holder of the cheque an amount of money from a specified current account.

■ A cheque is not *legal tender* although it is usually accepted as *money*. If it is signed on the back it becomes negotiable. If it is crossed by two lines with account payee it can only be paid into another account. Without these two lines, the cheque can be cashed.

Chicago School: an influential group of economists from Chicago University, including *Milton Friedman* and *Friedrich Hayek*, whose main tenets include *free markets, positive economics,* monetarism and minimal government.

CIF: the cost of insurance and freight which is included in the value of goods on the official *balance of payments*.

■ The same acronym can also mean 'charged in full'.

circular flow of income: the money flow that is passed through the economy in one direction while the flow of products is in the opposite direction.

■ A model of the circular flow in its simplest form shows the flows of income and expenditure between households and firms while more complex models include withdrawals in the form of savings, taxation and imports, and injections in the form of investment, government expenditure and exports.

classical economics: the contribution of early economists, such as *Adam Smith* (1723–1790), *Thomas Malthus* (1766–1834), Jean Baptiste Say (1767–1834), *David Ricardo* (1772–1823), and *John Stuart Mill* (1806–1873), to explaining how an economy allocates resources.

■ These classical economists were concerned with understanding markets, development and growth mainly from a microeconomic perspective, although they did recognise market failure and the need to make policy recommendations.

clearing cheque: a number of banks add up claims on each other, agree offsetting claims, and settle outstanding debts.

■ Traditionally, the London clearing house dealt with this on a daily basis for the main commercial banks. However, this service is gradually being replaced by electronic clearing systems.

closed economy: where the economic activity in certain economic models is analysed domestically without any assumed trade in international markets.

club good: a good which has the characteristics of both a *public good* and a *private good*.

▧ Inside the club the product is non-rival and non-excludable, whilst outside it is rival and excludable.

▧ *e.g.* Inside a theatre, disco or football match, people cannot be excluded from enjoying the entertainment. However, those outside are excluded.

Coase, Ronald: a British economist who was awarded the Nobel prize in economics in 1991 for his work on *externalities* and the theory of the firm.

▧ Coase's theorem states that externalities do not give rise to resource mis-allocation if property rights are clearly identified and there are no transaction costs. Producers and consumers trade potential externalities to their mutual benefit.

▧ *TIP* Many of the world's environmental problems may be the result of unclear or unenforceable property rights, e.g. over-fishing, over-whaling, destruction of hardwood forests, global warming.

cobweb theorem: a dynamic theory of *price* that recognises a time-lag between decision and execution such that a decision to produce a certain quantity is based upon the price prevailing in a previous production run.

▧ The theory is often illustrated by reference to the agricultural industry where farmers plant for the next harvest using price information from the previous harvest. The variable nature of supply can start a pattern that looks like the cobweb as illustrated below. Suppose a bad harvest produces Q_1 which sells at P_1. This induces Q_2 at the next harvest. Q_2 sells for P_2 and induces Q_3, and so on.

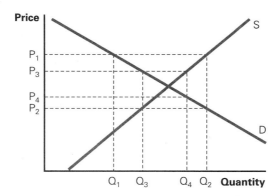

▧ Assuming there are no further unexpected harvests, the price and quantity eventually settle at the equilibrium.

▧ *TIP* To produce a stable cobweb that moves towards equilibrium, the value of supply elasticity must be less than the demand elasticity. If the supply and demand curves cross at 90°, an equilibrium can never be achieved, while a demand curve which is more inelastic than the supply curve produces an unstable cobweb that moves away from equilibrium.

coin: a definitive amount of metal whose weight and fineness are guaranteed by the official stamp of the issuing authority.

■ Originally, precious metals such as gold and silver were often minted into coins under the direction of the monarch. There was, however, always a temptation to debase the coinage by replacing precious metal with base metal. Henry VIII debased the coinage so much that between 1543–1547, 86% of the original metal was replaced. Once merchants realised this, they demanded more coins to make up the original amount of silver, which meant prices rose. A crude technique for checking the quality of coins was to bite them. See also *Gresham's law*.

collective bargaining: negotiations with an employer on behalf of all the employees regarding conditions of work and rates of pay.

■ The alternative to collective bargaining is each employee bargaining individually with the employer.

collusion: a form of agreement between firms to avoid damaging each other through individual price, output or marketing policies.

command economy: see *centrally planned economy*.

commercial bank: a private sector bank that accepts deposits and offers a transmission service for payments as well as savings, investment and loan facilities to individual customers.

■ Today, commercial banks offer a wide range of other financial services including mortgages, insurance, broking and business banking.

commodity: in its narrow sense this term refers to raw materials and foodstuffs.

■ Commodities are usually homogeneous. For example, it is difficult to distinguish between wheat produced by one farmer or another. There are many commodity exchanges throughout the world, e.g. wool, rubber, coffee, tea, sugar and oil.

■ *TIP* The term commodity also has a more general usage when it describes any good as opposed to a service.

Common Agricultural Policy (CAP): a price support system for farmers in the *European Union* that establishes a minimum price at which their products can be sold.

■ When the minimum price is higher than the market clearing price, surpluses are produced giving rise to so-called wine lakes and butter and beef mountains. Such products are also protected from international price shocks by export subsidies and import levies.

■ *TIP* CAP is an example of how political decisions may be taken without a real understanding of economics. The benefits to EU farmers, particularly inefficient ones, are offset by the enormous costs incurred by resource misallocation and administration. It also operates against the interests of consumers in Europe and farmers and consumers worldwide.

common external tariff: a uniform tariff applied by members of a customs union on chosen products imported into that union.

■ The aim is to replace different tariffs on the same import that existed in each country before the union was established.

common market: where a group of countries agrees to form an economic union which allows free trade and free movement of productive factors within the union and establishes a customs union with a *common external tariff*.

■ Common markets can go further and harmonise legal, social and welfare arrangements as well as transportation and communication networks.

■ *e.g.* European Union.

comparative advantage: a theory of trade, attributed to *David Ricardo*, which states that there can be gains from trade even when a country does not have an absolute advantage in the production of a product as long as there are different *opportunity costs* of production.

■ *e.g.* Suppose countries A and B both produce two products, wheat and barley, and given the same amount of resources, can produce the following totals:

	Wheat	Barley
A	75,000	100,000
B	50,000	80,000

Country A has *absolute advantage* in the production of both products, but if the opportunity costs of producing one unit of wheat and barley in each country are calculated, country A has the lower opportunity cost of producing wheat, while B has the lower opportunity cost of producing barley:

	Wheat	Barley
A	4/3B	3/4W
B	8/5B	5/8W

If each country specialises by allocating some more or all of its resources to the product with the lower opportunity cost, both countries benefit from trade even though country B only has a comparative advantage in the production of barley.

Competition Commission: an independent administrative tribunal that replaced the Monopolies and Mergers Commission to oversee UK competition policy and enforce the *monopolies, mergers and restrictive practices acts*.

complementary products: goods or services which are in joint demand. This means that a change in the price of one product affects the demand for the other product.

■ *e.g.* A fall in the price of compact disc players increases the demand for CDs, while a rise in the price of video recorders reduces the demand for video cassettes.

■ *TIP* The cross elasticity of demand calculation for complementary products is always negative.

concentration ratio: a percentage measure of total market sales achieved by a specified number of firms in that market.

▓ In the UK, three or five firms are commonly used in the measure while four firms tend to be the norm in the US.

▓ *TIP* Concentration ratios are one of several measures of the degree of monopoly power in an industry.

congestion cost: when an increase in the number of users imposes a cost on current users.

▓ This cost is an externality as it is not contracted, but its valuation is important in *cost–benefit analysis.*

▓ *e.g.* Congestion costs are an important part of transport policy analysis and are often included as an example of an external diseconomy of scale.

conglomerate firm: usually a holding company which owns a diverse group of unrelated businesses.

▓ A conglomerate usually develops as a firm grows through *merger* and acquisition in a bid to diversify and reduce the risk inherent in specialising in one product.

conspicuous consumption effect: see *snob effect.*

constant prices: used in certain economic measures so that distortions caused by nominal changes in the value of *money* are removed from the calculation and a measure of *real* changes in the economy can be identified.

constant returns to scale: when a firm adds *factors of production* in the same proportion and there are constant additions to total output.

consumer: a person (or group of people) who buys and/or uses a product.

▓ In microeconomic theory, the consumer is the smallest economic unit on which models are built. Where the consumer is a household, the group decision may suppress individual wants such that consumer decisions can be analysed with reference to a social welfare function which includes all the members of the group.

consumer durable: an imprecise term for a product which is not immediately consumed in full but is used over a long period of time.

▓ *e.g.* Television, cooker, furniture.

consumer equilibrium: when a consuming unit buys a basket of products and, given a fixed income and specified time period, maximises satisfaction or total utility.

▓ In reality, rational consumers aim to maximise satisfaction from their purchases and, in theory, this can be represented by a point at which the marginal utility derived from the last unit of money spent is equal for all products consumed. This is written as:

$$\frac{\text{marginal utility of X}}{\text{price of X}} = \frac{\text{marginal utility of Y}}{\text{price of Y}} = \frac{\text{marginal utility of Z}}{\text{price of Z}}$$

consumer expenditure: the aggregate of all expenditure by consumers in an economy over a specified period of time.

▓ Consumer expenditure is an important component of aggregate expenditure/demand. Assumptions about its relationship to income are therefore significant in terms of the potential of macroeconomic models of the economy to make accurate forecasts.

consumer good: a tangible product bought and/or used at the level of final demand.

consumer sovereignty: when consumer response to changes in products and prices dictates the response of competing producers.

▩ Consumer sovereignty is an important part of competitive market theory as it determines how resources are allocated and reallocated to satisfy consumer demand.

▩ **TIP** The more firms there are in an industry, the greater the likelihood that the consumer is sovereign. This force is reduced in industries where there are a few firms and eliminated under pure monopoly where the producer is described as sovereign.

consumer surplus: the difference between the maximum amount of money a consumer is willing to pay for a product rather than go without it and the amount actually paid.

▩ **e.g.** Suppose an individual is prepared to pay £10 to buy the first unit of a product, £9 to buy the second unit, £8 to buy a third and £7 to buy a fourth. If the market price were £7, the consumer would buy four units costing $4 \times 7 = £28$. However, the consumer would have been prepared to pay $10 + 9 + 8 + 7 = £34$. Therefore, the consumer surplus is £6 $(34 - 28)$. In the marketplace, the shaded area represents the value of the consumer surplus as shown below.

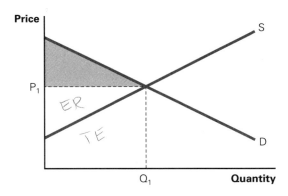

consumption function: the relationship between income and the amount of money spent on consumer products.

▩ This is an important function in building certain economic models and is usually referred to in its average and/or marginal form:

$$\text{average propensity to consume} = \frac{\text{total consumption}}{\text{total income}}$$

$$\text{marginal propensity to consume} = \frac{\text{change in consumption}}{\text{change in income}}$$

contestable market: a perfectly contestable market has no *sunk costs*, while the lower the sunk costs the more contestable the market.

▧ The theory of contestable markets implies that even in industries with only a few firms, as long as actual entry can take place or potential entry is anticipated, then firms produce at levels which achieve normal profits.

contractionary policy: reducing or slowing down the growth in *aggregate demand* when the economy is overheating or growing unsustainably fast.

▧ It may entail the use of monetary policy through an increase in the interest rate or a reduction in the money supply and/or fiscal policy where tax is raised or government expenditure is reduced.

▧ *TIP* Contractionary policy may be used to describe either an absolute decline in aggregate demand or a slowing down in the expected growth in demand.

convertible currency: a medium of exchange that can be freely converted, without limits, into other foreign currencies.

▧ In the past, a fully convertible currency has also been exchangeable into gold, but this characteristic is not required for a currency to be described as convertible in foreign exchange markets.

cooperative: a type of firm where the same group of people has both a financial interest and a say in how the firm is run.

▧ In a producer cooperative, the employees own and manage the firm and share the profits. In a retail cooperative, a group of independent retailers joins together to reduce individual costs through such things as bulk buying and joint advertising. In a consumer cooperative, a firm is run indirectly by the customers who have membership rights that may include dividends, voting rights and refunds on their shopping bill. In a financial cooperative, such as a credit union, deposits and loans are arranged between members of the union.

corporation tax: levied on the Inland Revenue's defined profits of a firm.

▧ *TIP* Because it is a tax on income, this tax does not affect the price or output structure of the firm. A change in corporation tax therefore does not affect the profit-maximising equilibrium. It is a common error, particularly in multiple-choice questions, for students to conclude that a change in this tax changes the price and output position of the firm.

cost–benefit analysis: a valuation of all the costs and benefits of a project where the total costs may include private and external costs, and the total benefits may include private and external benefits.

▧ Cost–benefit analysis provides a framework to appraise investment projects and is particularly useful in the public sector. Such an analysis may conclude that, despite an excess of private costs over private benefits and a project that would not be profitable in the private sector, a fuller analysis may indicate that total benefits exceed total costs and therefore society benefits if the project goes ahead.

▧ *e.g.* A private cost–benefit analysis of a proposed new ring road around a small town may show that costs exceed benefits. However, when externalities such as pollution and congestion are taken into account it may be that total benefits exceed total costs and the project creates an overall benefit for society.

■ *TIP* Questions involving cost–benefit analysis often stress the importance to society of a full evaluation of costs and benefits, but also recognise that it is often difficult to value externalities and, in some cases, even to decide whether an externality is a cost or benefit. It is also difficult to judge the rate of interest at which future costs and benefits should be discounted. If social time preferences are different from private time preferences, projects may go ahead in the public sector and displace more efficient private sector projects that have to achieve higher target rates of return.

cost–plus pricing (also called 'full cost pricing'): a theory of pricing which plays down the importance of supply and demand and suggests that firms use their costs plus a conventional mark-up to determine their profit margin and final selling price.

cost–push inflation: when a rise in the general (average) level of prices is caused by a significant rise in costs.

■ Costs may increase as the result of wage pressure, a desire to raise profit margins, a rise in import prices or any price rise which has a significant effect on the costs of production, e.g. energy prices.

■ *e.g.* Arguably, a significant period of worldwide cost–push inflation occurred as the result of oil price shocks in the early 1970s.

■ *TIP* An interesting point of discussion exists between Keynesians and monetarists. The Keynesians support the idea of cost–push inflation while the monetarists argue that inflation can only occur alongside a rise in costs if there is an accompanying rise in the money supply. Monetarists would therefore argue that the growth in money supply causes the inflation, not the rise in costs.

counter–cyclical policy: when a government adopts a strategy to stabilise an economy that works in the opposite direction to the prevailing destabilising fluctuation in economic activity.

■ *Keynes* was influential in getting governments to accept the idea of acting in a counter-cyclical way. He argued that when the economy is expanding too fast, the government should budget for a surplus to dampen down demand. On the other hand, when the economy is contracting, a budget deficit should be used to boost demand.

credit card: often referred to as plastic money, it is a card issued by a financial intermediary that enables the holder to obtain products on credit.

■ It is a common form of money used in transactions even though it is not *legal tender*. Credit cards vary from debit cards, which remove money directly from an individual's bank account, as they give the holder up to nearly 2 months of interest-free credit before the bill has to be settled.

■ *e.g.* In the UK, the two most common cards are Visa and Mastercard.

■ *TIP* If all credit cards were used in a cost-efficient way, no one would ever borrow on a credit card as there are cheaper forms of borrowing available. If this were to happen, the credit card companies would probably have to cease trading. Is this an example of consumers being irrational, or are they paying for the convenience of access to an easy loan?

credit controls: the various techniques available to the *Bank of England* for controlling the growth of lending and bank credit.

▦ Although there are various kinds of controls, e.g. open market operations, funding, quantitative control, qualitative guidance, special deposits, the Bank of England has only used interest rates as its policy option in recent years.

credit creation: the process by which the money supply is expanded when financial institutions make loans to customers on a fractional backing of cash or other liquid assets. See *bank credit multiplier*.

credit multiplier: see *bank credit multiplier*.

creeping inflation: small, but continuing increases in the yearly rate of inflation.

cross-price elasticity of demand: the responsiveness of demand for one product to the change in price of another product.

▦ The formula used to calculate cross-price elasticity of demand is:

$$\text{cross-price elasticity of demand} = \frac{\%\ \text{change in the quantity demanded of X}}{\%\ \text{change in the price of Y}}$$

▦ *e.g.* Products which are complements (CDs and CD players) and products in derived demand (cars and tyres) produce a negative answer as the rise in price of one product reduces the demand for the other product. Products which are substitutes for each other (Pepsi Cola and Coca-Cola) produce a positive cross elasticity as a rise in price in one product raises demand for the other product. If either the numerator or the denominator remain unchanged, the answer is zero or infinite, which usually indicates that the products are independent of each other.

▦ *TIP* A positive or negative cross elasticity produces a necessary though not sufficient condition for products being related. This is because changes could have taken place as the result of an unrelated coincidence. In addition, remember that a plus divided by a minus or a minus divided by a plus always produces a negative answer, whereas a plus divided by a plus or a minus divided by a minus always produces a positive answer.

cross subsidy: when an unprofitable part of the business is supported by a profitable part.

▦ *e.g.* A supermarket may sell popular products at a loss in order to encourage customers into the shop to buy other items on which it makes a profit.

crowding out: when a rise in investment or expenditure in the public sector reduces investment or consumption in the private sector.

▦ There is some debate among economists about the impact of crowding out at various levels of economic activity within the economy. Keynesians tend to accept crowding out at a level of full employment, but not if there are unemployed resources in the economy.

e.g. If a rise in investment in the public sector is financed through higher rates of interest, there is a corresponding reduction in private sector investment. If a rise in government spending raises the price of products and productive factors, then private production and consumption are reduced.

currency: a term often used to include the cash component of the *money supply,* i.e. notes and coins.

When used to denote a country's medium of exchange, e.g. sterling, dollar, franc, it refers to the total stock of money in a country.

currency appreciation: when a floating currency on foreign exchange markets rises in value against another or other currencies.

e.g. A rise in the value of sterling means that the same amount of UK currency buys more units of a foreign currency than before. In effect, the price of imports falls while the price of exports rises.

current account: a personal account held at a *bank* from which a customer can withdraw *cash*, make and receive payments using *cheques*, or transfer money to another account.

A positive balance in the account may or may not earn interest, and charges may or may not be levied on transactions through the accounts. A negative balance or overdraft incurs charges. Current or chequeable accounts are the largest component of the narrower money supply definitions.

TIP Do not confuse these accounts with the current account of the *balance of payments*.

customs duty: a tax levied on imported products.

This tax can raise revenue for the government, protect domestic industry, and be used selectively to direct customer preferences towards or away from products and countries.

customs union: an agreement between certain countries to trade freely amongst themselves and erect a *common external tariff* against non-member countries.

e.g. The *European Union* started as a customs union, although it now includes a wider range of agreements aimed at producing a single European market.

cyclical unemployment: when a downturn in the business cycle or trade cycle causes a loss of employment opportunities.

This is a short-term problem as demand soon picks up through the recovery phase of the cycle.

deadweight loss: the reduction in *consumer surplus* when a monopolist reduces output and raises price compared with a competitive industry; or the difference between the equilibrium position for an industry which excludes *externalities* and its *social optimum* if external costs and benefits are included.

debenture: fixed interest debts secured on the assets of the company.

■ The holder of a debenture is a creditor of the company, not an owner, and therefore has no voting interest in the company or claim on its profits. Debenture holders are paid irrespective of whether the firm is profitable of not.

debt problem: loans to less developed countries that they could not service or repay.

■ Early in the 1970s, western banks considered loans to less developed countries as safe lending. However, a significant rise in interest rates and a quadrupling of oil prices meant that many developing countries were unable to meet the terms of the debt. Many countries had to reschedule debts, others defaulted and, to this day, schemes for writing off debt are being considered.

debt rescheduling: when a country or firm cannot keep up with interest payments on a loan and is given a period of grace during which interest is added to the loan and new arrangements are made for servicing and repayment.

decision lag: the time lag between a decision being made and action being taken.

■ *e.g.* Decisions in monetary policy over changes in interest rates have very quick decision lags, while fiscal policy decisions require parliamentary debate and an Act of Parliament which makes the decision lag slower.

decreasing returns to scale: when the same proportional increase in all productive factors gives rise to decreasing additions to total output.

■ *TIP* This is a long-run phenomenon that should not be confused with the diminishing returns that eventually occur in the short run when variable factors of production are added to a fixed factor.

deficit: the negative balance when expenditure exceeds income.

■ A common reference in macroeconomics is made to the government deficit when tax is not sufficient to cover spending, or to the external imbalance when deficits exist on various accounts in the balance of payments.

deflation: there are two meanings: either a fall in the average level of prices where it is the opposite of *inflation*, or a reduction in the level of aggregate demand at the current level of prices where it is the opposite of *reflation*.

deflationary gap: the difference between the full employment level of productive capacity in an economy and a level of aggregate demand which determines a lower level of economic activity.

▤ *e.g.* It is commonly assumed in a Keynesian analysis of the economy that a deflationary gap can be closed by boosting aggregate demand.

deflator: a ratio of price indices used in *national income* statistics to remove the effect of price changes such that the figures can be interpreted as *real* changes in output. See *index number*.

▤ *e.g.*

	Year 1	Year 2
National income	1,000	1,100
Price index	100	102

Nominal national income has risen by 10%, average prices by 2%, therefore real national income has risen to:

$$\frac{1,100}{1} \times \frac{100}{102} = 1,078.43 = \text{a real rise of 7.8\%.}$$

deindustrialisation: the absolute or relative decline of manufacturing industry compared to the provision of services in an economy.

▤ *TIP* A debate exists between some economists who consider this a problem and others who consider it as part of a progression towards a richer, more advanced knowledge-based society.

demand (also called 'effective demand'): when a consumer has both the desire and the ability to purchase a product.

demand curve: the functional relationship between a change in price and a change in the quantity demanded of a product.

▤ It is conventional to illustrate this function with price on the vertical axis and quantity on the horizontal axis. The normal shape for a demand curve is downward sloping from left to right as illustrated below, although there are special cases of an upward-sloping curve. See *Giffen good*.

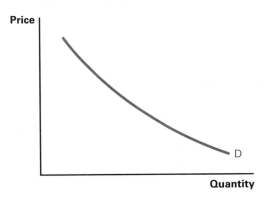

demand curve for labour: the functional relationship between changes in the wage rate and changes in the quantity of labour demanded. See *marginal revenue product curve*.

demand deficient unemployment: when the level of *aggregate demand* in an economy is not sufficient to employ all those people seeking employment.

■ This is essentially a Keynesian concept that requires an increase in aggregate demand to achieve full employment. However, the alternative view of the classical economist is that unemployment is due to wage rigidity in the short term which is eroded over the longer term as wages fall and more people are employed.

demand deposit: see *sight deposit*.

demand management: the management of *aggregate demand* using fiscal and monetary policy to achieve the main goals of macroeconomic policy, i.e. full employment, low inflation, a strong balance of payments and economic growth.

■ *TIP* There is considerable discussion about whether demand management is capable of achieving the aims set out above. Keynesian economists support policies which aim to achieve these targets through manipulation of aggregate demand, while other economists argue that it is supply-side policies that are proactive and demand-side policies that must be aimed at producing a stable level of average prices.

demand–pull inflation: a rise in the average price level in an economy which is caused by too much money chasing too few products.

■ In Keynesian analysis this is one of several causes of *inflation* and it can only occur at full employment when a rise in aggregate demand cannot be met with a rise in output. Monetarists, however, believe it is the only cause of inflation in that whenever inflation is recorded it must be the result of too much money chasing too few goods. If there are unemployed resources, then Keynesians usually explain inflation through *cost–push inflation* causation.

demerit good: a product which has rival and excludable characteristics but, when left to a free market, is likely to be overconsumed.

■ This is because consumers may not be aware of the potential damage to themselves and society of overconsumption; or, if aware, they may not be able to reduce consumption through addiction to the product.

■ *e.g.* Alcohol, cigarettes and gambling.

denationalisation: see *privatisation*.

dependency ratio: the ratio of people who are unable to work divided by those who are able to work.

■ Its significance is in a relatively crude observation that those who are working to produce goods and services are supporting not only themselves but also those who are not working. As an economy matures, so more people seem to be supported by a shrinking workforce. Whether or not this is a problem makes for an interesting debate.

depletable resource: a finite resource that once used up, cannot be replaced. See *non-renewable resource*.

d

▓ The definition includes fossil fuel which has taken millions of years to form but, given the current rate of usage, could be used up within this century. It also includes resources like hardwood forests which could be replaced, but not at the current rate of use.

▓ *TIP* There is a debate between economists who require intervention or foresee economic disaster as the main energy resources are used up, and economists who argue that the *price mechanism* allocates these resources efficiently until they are replaced by sustainable alternatives.

depreciation of capital: the rate at which capital value is reduced over time.

▓ There are two components of depreciation in the form of wear and tear, and obsolescence. Wear and tear is the result of *capital* being used up in the production process, while obsolescence occurs when alternative, more efficient forms of capital become available. Depreciation in the value of a machine can take place through obsolescence even when the capital is not being used.

depreciation of currency: the rate of exchange of one currency for another currency falls which means that the same quantity of the depreciated currency buys less foreign currency.

▓ *TIP* It is usual to use the term depreciation when the exchange rate falls in a floating system. In a fixed exchange rate system it is usual to refer to the devaluation of a currency when it is lowered to a new fixed level. The opposing movement to a depreciation in the price of a currency is an *appreciation*.

depression: a prolonged period of negative economic growth, high unemployment, falling prices and reducing incomes.

▓ *e.g.* The *Great Depression* of the 1930s.

deregulation: the removal of rules, regulations and laws which have been judged to impose restrictions on competition.

▓ *e.g.* Deregulation of energy provision and bus and rail services. The Big Bang in 1986 refers to City of London deregulation when it was opened up to international competition and a rigid job demarcation was relaxed.

derived demand: where the demand for a productive factor or component depends upon the final demand for a product.

▓ *e.g.* The demand for tyres is dependent on the demand for cars, while the demand for doctors is dependent on the demand for health services.

deterioration: see *wear and tear*.

devaluation: the reduction in the central price of one currency to a lower fixed level relative to other currencies under a *fixed exchange rate*.

▓ *TIP* Although devaluation stresses a movement from one fixed rate to another, students should recognise that market forces still determine the exchange rate. It is intervention in the buying and selling of currency by the central bank that sustains the fixed rate. When a central bank's foreign currency reserves are not sufficient to support the currency, then it is likely to be devalued.

developing country: a country with immature secondary and tertiary industries and an inability to finance its own investment in these sectors.

Countries with less than 20% of the per capita income of the US have been put into this category. They are often countries with a *debt problem* as well as a dependence on one or a few volatile primary industries. Their living standards are often sustained by foreign aid.

diminishing marginal returns: a law alternatively named 'the law of variable proportions' which states that when additional units of a variable factor of production are added to a fixed factor then — at some level of input of the variable factor — additions to total output will begin to diminish.

TIP This is a law about the short run as at least one factor of production is fixed. Although it is not part of the law, it is likely that increasing marginal returns to output precede diminishing marginal additions as variable factors are added.

diminishing marginal utility: a law which states that if a consumer buys additional units of the same product during a specified time period, the additions to total utility from each successive unit consumed will diminish.

This means that after the first unit consumed, total utility rises by diminishing amounts and could become negative if the consumer acted irrationally or had imperfect information about the effect of marginal consumption.

TIP It is a common mistake to assume that marginal utility rises before it falls. Remember, each marginal unit consumed may add the same or add less to the total utility.

direct tax: a payment made out of the income or wealth of individuals or the income (profits) of a firm to the Inland Revenue.

The burden of a direct tax falls upon the person paying whereas *indirect tax* or expenditure tax usually produces a shared burden between the producer and consumer.

e.g. Income tax, corporation tax, capital gains tax, capital transfer tax.

dirty float: describes a floating exchange rate system where intervention buying and selling of currency to support government policy takes place unexpectedly without any explanation.

A clearer strategy for intervention buying or selling to maintain the currency within certain limits or iron out daily fluctuations is referred to as a *managed float*.

discount market: where assets, with a guaranteed future value, are bought and sold at less than their face value representing a discount rate to the holder.

In its narrower sense discount market refers to the London discount market which has a special position in the UK financial system. Discount houses finance their purchases of *Treasury bills* and commercial or trade bills by borrowing from the commercial banks at relatively low rates of interest with a promise to return funds in cash if the banks find themselves short of cash. The market includes acceptance houses that guarantee the maturity value of trade bills. The discount market is much less important now that the *Bank of England* has ended the privileged position of discount houses and opened up dealing in short-term money market instruments to a wider range of financial institutions.

discount rate: the difference between the current price of an asset and its guaranteed future value.

- It is equivalent to the rate of interest that can be earned on savings products. This term is often used to describe the rate at which the *Bank of England* lends to commercial banks that have temporary liquidity problems and cannot meet their demands for cash.
- *e.g.* If a *Treasury bill* has a value of £100 in 3 months' time and the current rate of interest is 4%, then the bill will be purchased for approximately £99, earning approximately 1% over 3 months or 4% at an annualised rate.
- *TIP* Note that interest rates and discount rates are usually quoted over 1 year, therefore any rate for less than a year needs to be annualised.

discretionary policy: actions taken by a government to adjust levels and rates of taxation and expenditure in pursuit of its fiscal policy.

- In contrast, automatic adjustments can take place in taxation and expenditure as the result of changes in employment levels and inflation and growth rates (see *automatic stabiliser*).

discriminatory pricing: a producer, usually a monopolist, can separate the market into segments which have different price elasticities of demand and charge different prices in each part of the market.

- In order to do this, the firm must be able to stop resale between the markets. Perfect price discrimination means that each person is charged different prices for each additional product consumed and the consumer surplus is eliminated for every customer.
- *e.g.* Discrimination by age for cinema tickets, by sex for discos, by type of user for electricity and gas, and by time of the day for users of telephones and railways.
- *TIP* It is a common mistake to assume that all monopolists can price discriminate. This is incorrect as stopping resale is a precondition that only applies in a limited number of cases. Also, in some cases, it is possible to absorb the consumer surplus of richer customers to offer a service to poorer customers and still remain profitable even when a single price would cause a firm to make a loss.

diseconomies of scale: when firms grow too large and events inside or outside the firm cause the unit or average cost of production to rise.

- Inside the firm, internal diseconomies of scale can result from problems in managing a large workforce. Difficulties with communication, maintaining efficient control and worker motivation can raise average costs. Outside the firm, its growth and further expansion of the industry can lead to external diseconomies of scale as competition for a limited number of productive factors raises costs, and also congestion on the roads raises the cost of transport.

disequilibrium: an imbalance between *supply* and *demand* in a market, *aggregate supply* and *aggregate demand* in an economy, or the supply of exports and the demand for imports on the *balance of payments*.

▧ In static models of the economy there is a clear distinction between a state of rest or balance and a state of imbalance. Realistically, in a dynamic economy, variables are changing all the time so it is likely that imbalance exists more often than balance, and the best that can be said is that markets and the economy tend to move towards an ever-changing equilibrium.

▧ *e.g.* Within markets, a surplus of unsold products produces a disequilibrium, while in the economy as a whole, inflation, deflation and unemployment are measures of disequilibrium. Finally, between economies, deficits or surpluses on the accounts of the balance of payments signal disequilibrium.

disguised unemployment: this refers to people who are not registered for benefits and who therefore are not identified in unemployment statistics.

▧ This occurs when one partner in a relationship becomes unemployed but does not register. It can also occur when potentially unemployed people have been reclassified and removed from the official statistics. Some categories of unemployed people are not eligible for benefit and are offered no incentive to register.

disinflation: a fall in the measured rate of *inflation* when prices are still rising but by reduced amounts.

▧ *TIP* Disinflation should not be confused with a fall in the average level of prices which is usually referred to as *deflation*.

disintermediation: the breakdown of systems where funds flow to users via *financial intermediaries* like banks, brokers and building societies.

▧ The new systems of direct trade between a provider and a user, particularly through the Internet, bring closer contact and reduce the stages of intermediation in financial markets.

disinvestment: when capital stock used up in the production process is not replaced.

disposable income: what is left over to spend after a person's total income is reduced by claims in the form of taxation, national insurance and pension provision.

dissaving: a situation where a person, or an aggregate of people, spend more on consumption than can be financed from current income and therefore use up past savings.

▧ In a wider sense, dissaving is described as consumption greater than income where the gap is made up not only from savings but also from borrowings against future income or wealth.

distribution of income: the spread of total income shared among individuals or groups.

▧ Recognition of an uneven distribution of income has led to government using taxation and expenditure policies to bring about a more equitable distribution of income.

▧ *TIP* A debate revolves around whether more or less equality of income would be beneficial to the economy. One side of the argument points out that a more equal distribution of income raises economic welfare, while the other side points out that a more unequal distribution of income raises economic growth.

distribution of wealth: the spread of total wealth owned by individuals and groups.

This distribution is much more uneven than the distribution of income and therefore prompts political debate about how to create more equality. The problem is that if a tax system was based on redistributing wealth, then its success eliminates the source of the tax.

TIP A common mistake often made by non-economists is to argue for a redistribution of wealth when they really mean income. A vigorous debate exists between those who argue that it is essential in a modern society to have a more equal distribution of wealth and those who say that the distribution of wealth is unimportant and can be ignored because it derives such a small proportion of total income.

dividend: the reward to the shareholders of a company, usually paid out of current profits and fixed as a percentage of the historic price.

e.g. A 15p dividend on a £1 share = 15%.

dividend yield: the dividend per share in a company expressed as a percentage of the market price.

It shows the actual current return on shares and changes to reflect different market prices.

e.g. If the current market price of a £1 share is £3 and the dividend is 15p, then the dividend yield is 15p/300p × 100 = 5%.

division of labour: the break down of a production process so that each person can specialise in one part of that process and, through skill development and timesaving, workers' productivity is increased.

e.g. *Adam Smith* in ***The Wealth of Nations*** pointed out that the making of pins required 18 distinct operations and if one person did them all, approximately 20 pins would be produced each day. However, if ten people carried out some of the operations, then — through a division of labour — upward of 48,000 pins or 4,800 pins per worker would be produced each day.

TIP Despite the advantages set out above, it is recognised that the repetitive nature of these jobs can demotivate and alienate the workforce. Therefore, in order to enrich the working environment, many companies have tried to develop machines to do the repetitive jobs and create a more varied and interesting environment for their workers.

divorce of ownership and control: where shareholders have little interest in running the company, and managers are less concerned with profit-maximisation and more interested in the size and status of the company.

In these companies, the managers' salary may be linked to the size of the company and, as long as the company makes sufficient profits to satisfy the shareholder, those in control may expand the company past its profit-maximising level of output. This problem has obviously been recognised because many large companies insist that their top managers hold a significant number of shares so that their income is linked to the profitability of the company.

double coincidence of wants: a person offering a product must not only find someone who wants it, but someone offering what they want to receive in exchange.

■ This requirement is one of the main disadvantages of *barter*.

double counting: the same value is counted more than once as a result of being measured at different stages in the production process.

■ *e.g.* Firm A sells components valued at £800 to firm B which assembles them and sells them for £1,000. If the sales of both firms are added together then the total is £1,800, but this double counts £800 of components. The total value of output is £800 (firm A) + £200 (firm B) = £1,000.

dumping: when a product is offered for sale in another country at a price below its cost of production.

■ The aim may be to break into a new market and destroy the competition, or to sell off a surplus that cannot be sold domestically without damaging the local pricing structure, or to generate an inflow of foreign currency.

■ *TIP* In a world that promotes free trade, protection against dumping is usually accepted as an economic reason for import controls.

duopoly: a special case of *oligopoly* with only two firms in the industry.

■ Most theories of duopolistic behaviour concentrate on the overt and covert opportunities to collude and make *excessive profits*, although game theorists tend to conclude that duopolists are forced into a competitive equilibrium with *normal profits*.

duopsony: a special case market structure where there are only two buyers in the market.

dynamic economics: a branch of economics that recognises the thread of time that passes through the economy and therefore constructs economic models that include time-lags and variables that may be dated in time periods different from the present.

■ Static economic analysis produces models that are easier to understand but do not reflect reality and its complexity. Dynamic models are a step closer to reality but require more advanced analytical techniques.

ECB: see *European Central Bank.*

economic development: the process of raising real *per capita* income.

▨ Although the term can be applied to all countries, it is usually used to describe *developing countries* in the early stages of industrialisation.

economic efficiency: includes the two conditions of *productive* (technical) *efficiency*, where all firms produce at the lowest point on their long-run average cost curve, and *allocative efficiency* where firms produce at a level of output that equates price with marginal cost.

▨ Sometimes a third condition is added which refers to the optimal use of factor inputs and this produces a *pareto optimum* where no one can be made better off without someone else becoming worse off.

▨ *TIP* It is necessary to read questions on efficiency carefully, as a reference to economic efficiency requires at least an explanation of productive and allocative efficiency while other questions can ask for an explanation of either one or the other.

economic good: a product that is scarce and requires an allocative mechanism.

▨ In this context the reference to a *'good'* also includes services, and the reference to 'economic' excludes *free goods*.

economic growth: an increase in the *per capita* productive capacity of an economy.

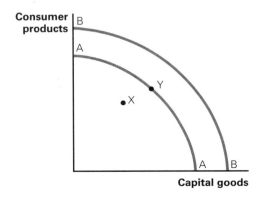

If we assume that an economy has a productive potential represented by the boundary AA in the diagram, then a shift in the boundary to BB is economic growth. On the other hand, if the economy is producing inside the boundary at X with unemployed resources, then output can expand towards the boundary at Y. However, this growth in output is not economic as there has not been a shift in the boundary.

economic model: a simplification of reality designed to impart some level of basic understanding of a system which is too complex to comprehend in its entirety.

Models can be very basic, as with the construction of supply and demand curves to determine equilibrium price and output, or they can be very complex attempts to model the whole economy using many more variables and making many more assumptions. The success of economic models is often judged by their ability to forecast future events. However, the thread of time passing through these events always produces uncertainty.

economic problem: the formal way of saying there are not enough resources available to satisfy all human needs and wants.

Fundamental to the study of economics is the fact that resources are scarce and therefore need an allocative mechanism. In a market economy, the economic problem means that there are insufficient resources to satisfy consumer *demand* at zero price.

TIP Do not confuse the economic problem with economic problems like *inflation* and *unemployment* which are symptoms rather than causes of *scarcity*.

economic rent: the surplus reward to any factor of production over and above its *transfer earning*.

e.g. If a professional footballer earns £20,000 a month and his next most lucrative employment is £2,000 a month, then he earns an economic rent of £18,000 a month. Alternatively, if the next best alternative foregone pays the same as the current reward then there is no economic rent.

TIP The structure of the reward to a productive factor is interesting because if an employer knew the breakdown between economic rent and transfer earning, then those factors employed with high economic rent could have their rewards reduced without risk of them leaving the firm. Fortunately, this information is not available.

economics: a study of the mechanisms used to allocate scarce resources to the production and exchange of *goods* and *services*.

The most commonly quoted definition comes from Lionel Robbins' influential work 'An essay on the nature and significance of economic science' (1935), in which he wrote that economics is 'the science which studies human behaviour as a relationship between ends and scarce means which have alternative use'.

economic welfare: that part of human welfare which is concerned with the consumption of goods and services.

Theoretically economic welfare can be increased if less money is spent on defence and more money on consumer products. *Redistribution policies* which take money away from the rich and give it to the poor raise economic welfare if the satisfaction lost by high income groups is less than the gain made by low income groups. The issues are, however, not quite so simple because, over time, a country may become less able to defend itself or *economic growth* may be slowed by redistributive policies.

economies of scale: when a firm grows larger and factors inside or outside the firm cause the unit or average cost of production to fall.

■ The firm's internal economies of scale result mainly from technical, marketing and financial economies. Outside the firm, external economies result from such things as local colleges offering training courses, government improvements to the local infrastructure or a component supplier moving nearby and thus reducing transport costs and delivery times.

economy: a term which encompasses all the economic activities that take place inside a national boundary.

effective demand: see *demand.*

EFTA: see *European Free Trade Area.*

elasticity of demand: the responsiveness of quantity demanded to a change in either price (*price elasticity of demand*) or income (*income elasticity of demand*) or, in the case of related products, to a change in the price of another product (*cross-price elasticity of demand*).

■ If the response of demand is proportionately greater than the change in the independent variable, then the calculation is greater than one and is described as elastic. If the response is proportionately less, it produces a calculation that is less than one and is described as *inelastic.*

elasticity of supply: the responsiveness of the quantity supplied to a change in product price.

Quantity supplied

■ The formula most commonly used is:

$$\text{elasticity of supply} = \frac{\%\ \text{change in quantity supplied}}{\%\ \text{change in price}}$$

■ If the response of supply to a change in price is proportionately greater, then the calculation is more than one and the description is elastic. If the response of supply is proportionately less, then the calculation is less than one and the description is inelastic.

■ *TIP* A common error is to identify unitary elasticity (where quantity supplied and price change by the same percentage) as a 45° angle line only. In fact, any straight line which passes through the origin of the graph has this characteristic as illustrated on p. 41.

emerging market: a reference to countries which have recently adopted a more market-focused approach to trade and industrialisation.

■ *e.g.* Some countries have linked economic freedom to political freedom e.g. Russia, while others have not offered political freedom, e.g. China.

emissions trading: a response to legislation in the US where firms which have been given or bought the right to release a certain level of pollutant gases into the atmosphere, sell on those rights to other companies.

■ This process internalises the external cost to society of pollution and, by placing a price on pollution, reduces the emission of gases into the atmosphere, ideally to a level which can be absorbed and cause no damage to the environment.

empirical testing: using real data or facts to test *economic models* and *forecasts*.

endogenous variable: a variable that can change from inside the model in question.

■ *e.g.* In the model of the *circular flow of income*, consumption is an endogenous variable, whereas an injection such as investment is an *exogenous variable*.

Engel curve: plots the relationship between a change in income and a change in the individual's consumption of a product.

■ For a *normal product* the curve is positive while for an *inferior product* it is negative. The slope of the curve is the ratio of a change in consumption to a change in income and therefore illustrates the *marginal propensity* to consume.

■ *e.g.* In the diagram below the product is normal when income starts to rise, but becomes inferior at income level Y_1.

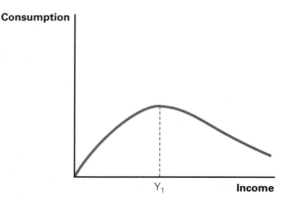

enterprise: one of the four *factors of production* — along with capital, land and labour — which coordinates the activities of the other factors. See *entrepreneur.*

entrepreneur: a person who brings together the productive factors, finances the productive process, and takes the uninsurable risks and uncertainty associated with business.

■ Small firms, including sole traders, usually possess the traditional entrepreneurial characteristics described above. However, in large firms, where there is a *divorce of ownership and control*, the financial risks are taken by the shareholders while control of the firm is in the hands of managers who may or may not be shareholders.

■ *TIP* There is a debate about whether entrepreneurship is a factor of production in its own right or just a specialist type of labour. Either way, there are further debates. On the one hand, there is the argument that entrepreneurs have done more towards solving the *economic problem* and promoting the development of civilisation than politicians. On the other hand, there is the image of entrepreneurs as greedy and self-seeking.

environmental degradation: a decline in the quality of the environment as a result of economic activities.

■ In many cases, this degradation is imperceptible over 1 year, but noticeable over many years. It prompts questions about our responsibility to future generations.

■ *e.g.* The *greenhouse effect*.

environmental economics: the branch of economics that looks at the total costs and benefits of economic activity, concentrating on *market failure, externalities* and property rights.

■ *e.g.* Pollution, congestion, over-use of non-renewable resources.

Equal Pay Act: introduced in 1970, it states that employers are required to give equal treatment to men and women.

■ The law applies where men and women are employed on the same, or broadly similar, work or, if the work is different, then the woman's job must be rated as equivalent to that of a man by means of a job evaluation exercise.

■ *TIP* This provides an interesting area for economic analysis, bearing in mind that the act was introduced in 1970 and became fully operational in 1975. Thirty years on there are claims that women still earn less than 80% of the men's wage in the same and similar jobs.

equilibrium: a state of balance between economic variables such that there are no forces of change to be set in motion.

■ Economic analysis commonly looks at this relationship from the point of view of supply and demand at the individual, market and aggregate levels. In static analysis equilibrium is studied as an end in itself, while in dynamic analysis equilibrium may not be achieved, but it gives direction to economic change.

equilibrium price and output: where, in simple static market analysis, the quantity demanded by consumers is equal to the quantity supplied by producers, and market forces are balanced in a position which is stable.

In the diagram below, P_1Q_1 represents equilibrium. A higher price at P_2 sets market forces in motion as a build up of stock causes firms to lower output and reduce prices to clear the surplus. A lower price at P_3 causes a shortage and firms can take advantage of this to raise prices, output and profits.

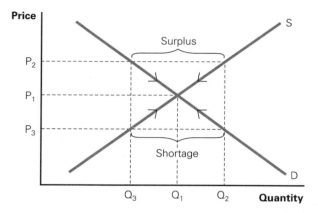

equi-marginal utility: states that a consumer maximises total satisfaction by equating the utility per unit of money spent on the marginal unit of each product purchased. See *consumer equilibrium*.

e-trade: alternatively known as e-commerce or e-tail (as opposed to retail).
■ This kind of trade is where products are sold via the Internet at competitive prices as a result of the savings involved in having a virtual site rather than a more expensive actual site.

EU: see *European Union*.

euro: the European currency unit to which the members of the *European Monetary Union* are irreversibly fixed.
■ January 1999 was the beginning of conversion to a single European currency which should be completed by 2002. The UK was not a founder member of this transition to the euro.

eurocurrency market: traders are domestic banks that accept deposits and make loans in a foreign currency.
■ The market started when US dollars were placed on deposit in Europe during the Cold War between America and the USSR. Subsequently, the market has developed to accept all the main internationally traded currencies in an environment that avoids domestic constraints on the currency. The name is now a misnomer as similar markets have developed throughout the world.
■ *TIP* Do not confuse this market, which deals in loans and deposits, with the foreign exchange market that deals in the buying and selling of foreign currency.

European Central Bank (ECB): the central bank of the *European Union* which was set up, alongside the introduction of the *euro*, to maintain stability and play a major role in establishing uniform interest rates throughout the EU.

European Free Trade Area (EFTA): this was set up in 1959 as a rival organisation to the *European Union* and included most of the non-EU European countries.

A *free trade area* differs from a *customs union* in that there is no common external tariff and each country can set its own barriers with the rest of the world. This situation gives rise to the need for a re-export tax which stops outside countries exporting to the country with the lowest tariff in the free trade area for distribution to other members. In 1991, EFTA and the EU moved into a closer affiliation when the two organisations allowed a free movement of products and productive factors between them.

European Union (EU): the latest name for the European Economic Community (EEC) which was set up as a *customs union* in 1957 by the Treaty of Rome and included Belgium, France, Germany, Italy, Luxembourg and Holland.

The UK joined in 1973 along with Denmark and Ireland. They were followed by Greece (1981), Portugal and Spain (1986) and Austria, Sweden and Finland (1995). Very soon after its inception, the EEC started to develop a uniform approach to a whole range of economic, social, legal and political criteria. By 1993, the EEC had established the structure for a Single European Market. It was renamed the European Union and, under the *Maastricht Treaty*, established the framework for a more federal Europe with its own currency, the *euro*. Not all countries adopted the euro in January 1999, but it is anticipated that all member countries will join sooner or later.

ex-ante: an epithet which describes the planned, expected or anticipated future event, whereas *ex-post* is a reference to what has already happened.

excess capacity: when a firm or firms are producing at a lower output than that required to achieve the lowest average cost of production.

Profit-maximising firms in *imperfect competition* do not reach capacity output which is the lowest point on their average cost curve. The excess capacity theory is used to explain how firms in *monopolistic competition* always produce in long-run equilibrium on the downward-sloping part of their average cost curve.

TIP Remember that excess capacity is below, not above, capacity output.

excess demand: when the price in a free market is below *equilibrium* and demand exceeds supply.

In *macroeconomics*, excess *aggregate demand* may lead to *demand–pull inflation*.

excessive profit (also called 'supernormal profit'): any level of profit above the *normal profit* which is required to keep the *entrepreneur* in a particular line of business.

TIP *Excessive profit* is sometimes referred to as an *abnormal profit*, which is correct, although the terms are not interchangeable as abnormal profit can also mean subnormal or less than normal profit.

excess supply: when the price in a free market is above *equilibrium* and supply exceeds demand.

In *macroeconomics*, excess *aggregate supply* may lead to a fall in the average level of prices and/or unemployment.

exchange equalisation account: held by the *Bank of England*, this includes foreign currency reserves, gold and sterling, to be used for stabilising the UK currency in foreign exchange markets in line with government policy.
- The account may just be used to iron out fluctuations in the exchange rate or it may be part of maintaining various exchange rate targets. To raise its price, sterling is bought using foreign currency. To lower its price, sterling is sold to buy foreign currency.

exchange rate: the price of a currency measured in terms of another currency.
- The rate may be determined in a free market through the forces of supply and demand, it may be influenced by government intervention in terms of buying and selling in the *foreign exchange market*, or it may be determined by government policy without reference to a market rate. In this third case there may be a considerable difference between the official rate and the unofficial market rate that leads to a *black market* for the currency.
- *TIP* When explaining the determination of an exchange rate in a free market, remember that the price of one currency can only be measured in terms of another. Therefore, to measure the price of sterling, the vertical axis must read dollars or another currency. The supply of a currency is determined by the demand for imports, and the demand for a currency is determined by the demand for exports.

excise duty: a tax collected by HM Customs and Excise which is usually a *specific tax* placed on products, although there can be an ad valorem element.
- *e.g.* A specific sum of money is placed upon alcohol, tobacco and petrol.
- *TIP* Specific taxes shift supply curves parallel to each other, while a percentage change in *ad valorem tax* shifts the supply curve with an increasing gap as the output increases, as illustrated below:

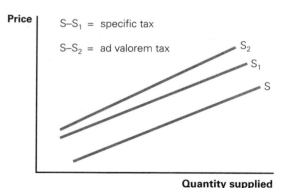

excludable: a characteristic where a producer can exclude consumers from using its product by charging a price that means those who cannot or will not pay the price are excluded from using the product.
- *Private goods* are excludable: see *rival*.
- *e.g.* Use of your camera or car is exclusive.

exogenous variable: a variable that changes the model in question from the outside.

■ *e.g.* In the model of the *circular flow of income*, withdrawals and injections are exogenous variables while consumption is an *endogenous variable*.

expansionary policy: government increasing *aggregate demand* by *monetary policies* that lower interest rates and/or raise the money supply, or fiscal policies that increase expenditure and/or reduce taxation.

expectations: what people anticipate will happen in the future.

■ This is interesting to economists because people's expectations may affect their current actions.

■ *e.g.* If people expect that inflation is going to rise, then they may bring forward purchases to take advantage of relatively lower prices in the present, or they may be encouraged to ask for a higher wage increase to compensate for expected higher prices. The current action is real even if the future event does not materialise.

expenditure reducing policy: a policy which reduces aggregate demand through contractionary monetary and/or fiscal policies.

expenditure switching policy: a policy which restructures the pattern of demand in the economy.

■ *e.g.* Such policies are commonly referred to in the context of *balance of payments* problems and may be used to try and reduce demand for imports and increase demand for domestic products. In this case, *devaluation* would be an expenditure switching policy.

expenditure tax: see *indirect tax*.

export-led growth: one of the policies, particularly relating to *developing countries*, which is aimed at taking the country out of poverty through generating income from overseas sales.

■ *e.g.* Japan's growth rate since 1945 is often explained as the result of adopting this policy.

exports: goods and services produced domestically but sold to residents of foreign countries.

■ In the balance of payments a distinction is made between visible goods that cross national boundaries and invisible services that may be used by foreigners in the domestic country, such as tourism, or used from the foreign country as with insurance services.

ex-post: an epithet which describes a realised or actual event that has happened, whereas *ex-ante* is the planned or anticipated future event.

external diseconomies of scale: events that occur outside the firm, usually when the industry is growing, that increase the unit or average cost of production of the firm.

■ *e.g.* Higher prices for *factors of production* or road congestion and increased travel times.

external economies of scale: events that occur outside the firm, usually when the industry is growing, that reduce the unit or average cost of production of the firm.

■ *e.g.* A local college may start offering courses to train workers, so reducing the firm's training bill; or new roads and motorways may be built that reduce travel time.

externality: a cost or benefit of either production or consumption which has spillover or third party effects that are not paid for by the producer or consumer.

■ Because externalities are not paid for, they are hard to measure and estimates of their valuation to society are not only difficult but are considered by some economists, who are particularly critical of *cost–benefit analysis,* to be impossible.

■ *e.g.* An external cost of production might be a discharge of waste into a river that kills the fish; an external benefit of production might be a discharge of waste into a river that feeds the fish; an external cost of consumption is car exhaust fumes; and an external benefit of consumption is a beautiful front garden.

■ *TIP* A common mistake is to refer to external production costs only as externalities. Remember that external production benefits or external consumption costs or benefits need to be considered in answering any question on externalities.

factor endowment: identifies the quantities and proportions of *land, labour, capital* and *enterprise* available to an economy or region.

■ The more developed countries have higher proportions of capital and entrepreneurial skills while the less developed countries have proportionately more labour and, in some cases — despite having significant land resources — may not have the capital and entrepreneurial skills to develop them.

factor incomes: the rewards to the *factors of production* from the output of goods and services.

■ Labour receives wages and salaries, land receives rent, capital receives interest and enterprise receives profit.

factor markets: where the interaction of supply and demand determine the rewards to the factors of production.

■ In a *free market*, supply and demand have a significant influence over factor income. However, there are market distortions, the most significant of which is government. In a *centrally planned economy* it is possible that rewards are totally unrelated to the potential market rewards.

factors of production: the elements necessary for economic production are traditionally subdivided into four groups: *land, labour, capital* and *enterprise*.

■ Land includes all the natural resources, while labour includes mental and physical effort. Capital is a produced means of production, and entrepreneurs organise the other factors into a productive unit and endeavour to make them profitable.

■ *TIP* Some textbooks refer to only three factors, preferring to categorise enterprise as a subgroup of labour. Also remember that land is more than just the ground you stand on. All the free gifts of nature — including the sea — are land resources in economics.

FDI: see *foreign direct investment*.

Federal Reserve: the American equivalent of the *Bank of England* is responsible for monetary policy, acting as lender of last resort, establishing the level and structure of interest rates, and setting the minimum reserve requirements for US banks.

■ The Federal Reserve Board is located in New York and there are 12 regional reserve banks that execute control on behalf of the Fed (common abbreviation).

The strength of the US economy is such that the Fed's decisions can make an impact throughout the world.

fiduciary issue: the part of the *Bank of England* note issue which is not backed by gold.

■ It was first recognised in the Bank Charter Act of 1844. Since 1939, when the government transferred all gold from the issue department of the Bank of England to the *foreign exchange reserves*, the whole note issue has been fiduciary.

financial capital: the liquid assets of a firm that are cash, or could quickly be turned into cash, and are distinct from physical capital.

financial intermediation: the process whereby funds flow from providers of financial products through intermediaries to the final user.

■ *e.g.* Banks accepting deposits and making loans, brokers acting between buyers and sellers of financial securities.

fine-tuning: a description, in Keynesian demand management policies, of the small adjustments in taxation and expenditure that eliminate fluctuations in economic activity and maintain *full employment*.

■ *TIP* The degree to which the economy can be fine-tuned is a matter of considerable debate and non-Keynesian economists suggest that many dynamic variables and unpredictable time-lags mean there is insufficient information to use fine-tuning policies effectively.

firm: a unit of production distinguished from other units by ownership.

■ A firm can range in size from a sole trader where one person owns, manages and works in the firm, to a multinational company which employs tens of thousands of people, and is owned by hundreds of thousands of shareholders and trades throughout the world. Theories of the firm range from the many-firm industry in *perfect competition* to the single-firm industry or *monopoly*.

■ *e.g.* Tesco in the food retailing industry, BMW in the car industry and Shell in the petroleum industry.

■ *TIP* Also note that a single firm can be active in several different industries, i.e. Virgin is active in trains, planes, financial products, music, retailing and broadcasting.

fiscal drag: the restraining effect on a boost to *aggregate demand* caused by a rise in taxation, which accompanies higher incomes and/or inflation.

■ It is particularly noticeable in a *progressive tax* system.

fiscal policy: government using taxation and expenditure to manipulate aggregate demand and influence the overall level of economic activity.

■ Before *Keynes*, governments had *budgets* but they did not use fiscal policy. After Keynes's ideas were adopted, governments felt empowered to act against the fluctuations in economic activity by stabilising the economy at full employment. This meant budgeting for a deficit when the economy was turning down to lower prices, incomes and unemployment, and budgeting for a surplus when the economy was expanding too rapidly and inflation was threatening.

TIP Keynesians consider fiscal policy as their most important tool of economic management, especially when it is used with an *accommodating monetary policy*. In contrast, monetarists consider monetary policy as all important and fiscal policy must be used to accommodate monetary targets.

Fisher, Irving (1867–1947): a mathematician turned economist whose significant contributions to the subject included capital value discounted in anticipation of future income, time preference and interest rates, the use of index numbers and, significantly, the *quantity theory of money.*

In the quantity theory of money Fisher used the equation $M.V = P.T$ to understand the relationship between money and the real economy. M is the stock of money, V is its *velocity of circulation*, P is the average price level and T is the number of transactions in a given time period. This analytical tool has undergone much development and adjustment, but still remains the foundation of modern monetary economics.

fixed costs: costs of production that remain the same at all levels of output including zero.

e.g. A firm may have to pay the rent and rates on its factory irrespective of how much it produces.

fixed exchange rate: an agreed rate at which the domestic currency is fixed against one or more foreign currencies.

The government agrees to maintain the exchange rate at or near this level through intervention buying and selling of the currency. It is usually stated that the currency can move either side of its par value by one or more per cent before intervention takes place. If not, the central bank would be intervening every minute of every day.

TIP In either a fixed or floating system it is necessary to understand that market forces determine exchange rates. The difference between the two is that under a fixed system the government intervenes by buying and selling the currency to maintain its rate.

fixed factors of production: these exist in the *short run* when the quantity used cannot be changed.

These fixed factors become variable in the *long run*.

e.g. Plant and machinery.

floating debt: part of the *national debt* which is made up of short-term debt (less than 1 year to maturity) and very short-term debt (90-day *Treasury bills*).

The floating debt can form part of a commercial bank's reserve assets and therefore the quantity of floating debt on the market can influence the money supply.

floating exchange rate: when a currency rate of exchange in the *foreign exchange market* is left to be determined by the free interplay of *market forces*.

It is unlikely that currencies will ever be totally free from government influence, and an intervention, depending on the degree of government openness, is known as a *managed float* or *dirty float*.

FOB: see *free on board*.

forecasting: making predictions about future economic events.

▨ These forecasts may be based upon simple extrapolations of past events or they may be deduced from more complex econometric models. There is a significant demand for economic forecasts and many economists and economic institutions make a living satisfying this demand. However, forecasts can in no sense be considered as certain and must therefore be viewed with a degree of scepticism and an acceptance of probability.

foreign aid: the transfer of funds from more developed countries to less developed countries in support of economic development and offered in a variety of ways including long-term loans, *soft loans*, technical aid and charitable gifts.

▨ There is considerable debate about whether foreign aid is an efficient way of raising living standards in less developed countries. 'Trade not aid' is a slogan of many developing nations that feel their economic growth is being hindered by trade barriers erected by the more developed world. An obvious example are the barriers surrounding the *Common Agricultural Policy*.

foreign direct investment (FDI): where firms in one country invest in factories and outlets in another country.

▨ This is different from buying shares in foreign firms which is an indirect form of investment.

▨ *e.g.* Japanese car manufacturers have built factories in Wales and northeast England.

foreign exchange: the currency of foreign countries.

▨ *e.g.* Dollars, francs, lira.

foreign exchange market: commonly known as the FOREX market, it is where all the main trading currencies of the world are bought and sold at spot (current) rates or at forward rates.

▨ Forward rates are an agreed price in the present for delivery of foreign currency on a specified date in the future. This provides traders with certainty regarding the future price of a currency and the forward market grows rapidly when currencies are floating and volatile.

▨ *TIP* Do not confuse the foreign exchange market with the *eurocurrency market*, where deposits are made and loans are offered in foreign currency.

foreign exchange reserves: currencies other than sterling held in the *exchange equalisation account* at the *Bank of England* to accommodate temporary imbalances in the *balance of payments*.

▨ When official financing is required to cover a deficit on the balance of payments the reserves fall, while a surplus causes foreign exchange reserves to increase.

forward integration: see *vertical integration*.

forward rates: see *foreign exchange market*.

franchising: when a successful business, with a strong brand, sells the right to copy the business for an initial fee, annual payments and a signed contract.

Limits are imposed on the franchisee including design of premises, use of suppliers and area of operation.

- Although commonly found in the private sector, government has used franchising for transport routes and the National Lottery.
- *e.g.* McDonald's, Pizza Hut.

freedom of entry/exit: one of the main characteristics of *perfect competition* that describes a situation where there are no barriers to firms entering or leaving a particular industry.

- It usually means that there are many small firms in the industry and no prohibitive start-up costs.

free good: a product which is in sufficient quantity to satisfy all demand without the need for an *allocative mechanism*.

- This means that the product is not scarce and does not require a market as supply equals demand at zero price.
- *e.g.* Air, sunshine, sea water.
- *TIP* Do not confuse this product with a good that may be provided free by government, like education. Also, although air is a free good, fresh air in a town like Los Angeles may have to be paid for and therefore becomes an economic good.

free market: where the competitive interaction of many producers and consumers, without any intervention by government, provides the forces of supply and demand to allocate resources through the *price mechanism*.

free on board (FOB): used in balance of payments statistics to denote that the valuation of products does not include the cost of insurance and freight (*CIF*).

free rider: a person who consumes a product without contributing to the cost of its production.

- One of the reasons that street lighting is referred to as a *public good* is that it is non-excludable, which means that free riders cannot be excluded from benefiting from its light and therefore they do not contribute freely to the costs of providing the service. The greater the opportunity for free riding, the more likely the product will have to be provided by government and financed through the compulsory removal of tax.

free trade: a situation of non-intervention by governments in the process of exchange which is often used to describe a flow of imports and exports across national boundaries.

- Theoretically, market forces and comparative advantage allocate resources efficiently and maximise national incomes throughout the world. In reality, this does not happen and barriers to trade are commonly erected and maintained by government.

free trade area: a group of countries agree to trade freely between themselves but maintain their own barriers with the rest of the world.

- *e.g.* European Free Trade Area.
- *TIP* Not to be confused with a *customs union* where free trade is agreed between

countries but there is an external *tariff* barrier which is common to all the members.

frictional unemployment (also called 'search unemployment'): a temporary state where a person registers as unemployed after leaving one job before starting another job.

■ It usually means that unemployed people and job vacancies exist at the same time in the same place.

Friedman, Milton (1912–): a leading monetarist economist, a member of the *Chicago School*, and winner of the 1976 Nobel prize for economics.

■ As well as developing the *quantity theory of money*, Friedman has been influential in arguing for a monetary structure from within which a free market economy can function efficiently with a minimum of government intervention. Other areas in which he has been influential include the idea of *human capital*, the *permanent income hypothesis*, the natural rate of unemployment, the relationship between *inflation* and unemployment and the methodology of *positive economics*.

full cost pricing: see *cost–plus pricing*.

full employment: Keynesian terminology for a level of employment where there are sufficient jobs available for all those people seeking work.

■ After 1945, many governments established a policy target for achieving full employment using *demand management* policy. It seemed to be successful until the 1970s, when manipulating *aggregate demand* arguably caused *inflation* rather than absorbing unemployed resources. Today, a policy target for full employment is not discussed by politicians, although it still remains a point of debate among economists.

funded debt: that part of the *national debt* which is made up of medium- and long-term debt securities including undated stock.

funding: the replacement of that part of the *national debt* which is floating or short term by longer-term securities or *funded debt*.

■ Because *floating debt* is a significant part of the reserve assets of commercial banks, the process of funding was an important way of controlling the *money supply*. However, in recent years, it has been much less important as monetary management is predominantly through adjustments to short-term interest rates.

gains from trade: these take place when countries specialise in producing those products for which they have an *absolute advantage* or a *comparative advantage* and then trade to satisfy relative consumer demand.

■ *TIP* When required to give an example of gains from trade, use comparative advantage which illustrates a higher level of understanding than absolute advantage.

Galbraith, John Kenneth (1908–): an influential economist and professor at Harvard University who questions whether a capitalist *free market* can work efficiently with only a minimum of government intervention.

■ Galbraith is a supporter of *Keynesian economics* and a critic of the *Chicago School*, the power of large firms, and the abuse of *advertising*. He is one of those rare economists who have written in a way that has attracted a significant readership among non-economists.

game theory: a model to explain outcomes when rational decisions are based on uncertainty and the imperfect knowledge of other peoples' actions and reactions.

■ In reality, firms have every incentive, in a competitive environment, to protect their knowledge and act in ways that surprise their competitors. This is the opposite of what is assumed under *perfect competition*.

■ *e.g.* The application of game theory to a *duopoly* produces the opposite conclusion from what might be expected according to traditional economic theory. Textbooks generally suggest that a two-firm industry is most likely to collude to make excessive profits. However, game theory predicts that because neither firm is certain about the other's action, they will be forced into a competitive situation where profits are normal rather than excessive.

GATT: see *General Agreement on Tariffs and Trade*.

GDP: see *gross domestic product*.

General Agreement on Tariffs and Trade (GATT): this came into effect in 1948 and was established to encourage countries to reduce or remove tariff and non-tariff barriers to trade.

■ In 1995 GATT turned into the *World Trade Organisation (WTO)* which has a wider brief to regulate the world trading environment while continuing to push for less restraint on international trade.

g

general equilibrium: where *aggregate demand* equals *aggregate supply* or where supply equals demand in each of the economy's many product and productive factor markets.

■ Analysis at the level of general equilibrium traces through the overall effect of change whereas *partial equilibrium analysis* uses the *ceteris paribus* assumption to limit the variables that can change.

Giffen good: a special case of an *inferior product* which has a strong negative *income elasticity of demand* such that when a price changes the income effect is opposite and greater than the substitution effect, producing a perverse demand curve.

■ Giffen goods are inferior products which form a significant part of the expenditure of poor people. Sir Robert Giffen (1837–1910) is credited with first identifiying that during the nineteenth century the poor of London consumed more bread when the price rose and less when the price fell. As the price of bread fell, so poorer people gained a significant increase in their spending power. This rise in real income encouraged them to purchase higher quality foodstuffs such as meat and dairy produce. These purchases reduced the demand for bread as consumers redistributed their diet in favour of superior alternatives, hence producing a demand curve that slopes upward from left to right.

gilt-edged security: a government debt, excluding *Treasury bills*, that can be bought and sold second hand on the *stock exchange*.

■ Originally gilt-edged was a reference to the stock certificates which were edged with gold leaf; now it is linked to the low risk of default compared with other types of security.

globalisation: the way in which a supranational economy is developing in the markets for both products and assets.

■ Some of this is under the control of government in the form of *trade liberalisation* and larger trading blocs. Some of it is developing out of government control where people are using the Internet to buy and sell products and assets using UK or foreign intermediaries.

■ *e.g.* Living in London and buying CDs in Los Angeles, or thinking of moving to Australia and contacting Australian estate agents and solicitors over the Internet.

GNP: see *gross national product*.

gold exchange standard: this replaced the gold standard as a managed way of maintaining international liquidity after the *Bretton Woods* conference established a fixed exchange rate throughout the trading world.

■ Countries could use US dollars as if they were gold and central banks could change official dollars into gold at a fixed rate.

gold standard: this developed throughout the eighteenth and nineteenth centuries in the UK when bank notes were freely convertible into and backed by gold.

▓ As international trade developed, so the gold standard was adopted internationally in settlement of debts. Countries in deficit on their balance of payments would settle their debt by transferring gold to the creditor country. In this way, domestic deflation and a foreign country reflation would maintain a fixed price for currency in international markets.

good: a tangible product that contributes to satisfying human wants and adds to *economic welfare*.

▓ Sometimes 'goods' is used as a collective noun which includes all products; alternatively, goods are separated from services which are intangible products.

▓ *e.g.* Car, chair, food.

▓ *TIP* Occasionally the term 'good' is used as an adjective that decribes an external benefit to society, and is opposite to a 'bad' which is an external cost to society.

Goodhart's law: named after the contemporary economist Charles Goodhart (1936–) who stated that if government sets a target for a monetary aggregate, then the process of choosing the aggregate distorts it such that the target is not achieved.

government: a group of people empowered to make decisions on behalf of the citizens of a country.

▓ A large proportion of decisions made by government directly or indirectly affects the economy.

▓ *TIP* Economists debate the degree to which government should be involved in economic management. At one extreme, a case is made for government doing little more than satisfying the collective demand for public goods. At the other extreme, a case is made for a centrally controlled economy. However, the real debate is about how close countries should move towards these extremes.

government expenditure: the current and capital expenditure of government, where current expenditure maintains the present level of services and capital expenditure adds to the level of services.

▓ Government expenditure is an important component of *aggregate demand* and a tool of economic management.

government failure: said to occur when intervention to correct *market failure* does not improve *economic efficiency*, or even reduces the efficiency with which resources have been allocated.

▓ Arguably, government becomes involved in trying to correct market failure for political reasons and does not have the information or expertise to improve upon the situation. Some economists have argued that it is rare for government to improve upon the market mechanism. Even in the case of *public goods*, it is not recognised that government does the job efficiently. It is just that the job would not be done at all without some form of intervention.

government security: a short-term, medium-term, long-term and undated debt sold by government to finance the deficit between government expenditure and taxation.

▓ *e.g. Treasury bill* and *gilt-edged security*.

g

gradualism: an approach to stimulating economic development that suggests the process is more likely to be successful if it is slow and steady.

■ The alternative approach is a shock or big push which recognises leaps forward rather than smooth growth.

Great Depression: the last true deflation which was characterised by a fall in the average level of prices.

■ It started after the 1929 Wall Street crash and spread through America and Europe, causing incomes to fall and unemployment to rise as much as 33% in America and Germany.

■ *TIP* There is an interesting debate about the cause of the Great Depression. *Galbraith* argues that the collapse of an overvalued stock market was the cause, while *Friedman* and Schwartz argue that it was the subsequent failure of the *Federal Reserve* to provide liquidity to the US banking system that brought about a series of bank failures and a monetary contraction.

greenhouse effect: the result of a build-up of carbon dioxide in the air through car exhaust fumes, industrial pollutants and deforestation, which is preventing solar heat from leaving the earth's atmosphere, causing global warming.

■ *TIP* There is an interesting debate between scientists, who point out only the damaging effects of global warming, and economists, who argue that possible benefits from global warming need to be put alongside the costs.

green pound: a fixed rate green pound is used to convert agricultural prices into domestic prices.

■ The fact that sterling floats against other European currencies, including the *euro*, produces daily adjustments to agricultural prices in a system where they should be fixed. However, a problem exists when the green pound and sterling diverge considerably over time and an eventual realignment of rates has to take place.

Gresham's law: formulated by Thomas Gresham (1519–79) at a time when money had an *inherent value* but was at risk of being debased, such that the bad money would drive out the good as people hoarded the money with the higher intrinsic value.

gross domestic fixed capital formation (also called 'gross investment'): the total investment in capital and infrastructure which includes replacement investment to cover depreciation and the new investment required to increase productive capacity.

gross domestic product (GDP): the total value of the output of an economy usually measured over 1 year.

gross investment: see *gross domestic fixed capital formation*.

gross national product (GNP): gross domestic product plus property income earned from investment abroad minus property income paid out to foreigners who own investments in the domestic economy.

Harrod–Domar growth model: Roy Harrod (1900–78) and Evsey Domar (1914–) produced one of the early growth models which included an accelerator investment function (see *accelerator theory*) and distinguished between the warranted rate of growth (produced from the model) and a natural rate of growth.

■ The model allows for growth at full employment and is sufficiently flexible to incorporate changes in technical progress and monetary variables, although it does assume a fixed rate of prices.

Hayek, Friedrich (1899–1992): a leading monetarist economist and a colleague of *Milton Friedman* at the *Chicago School*.

■ Hayek's early work focused on money and fluctuations in economic activity. His book, ***The Road to Serfdom*** (1944), was part of a continuing attack on interventionist economics and the centralisation of political power. Originally a member of the Austrian School, his glittering career included chairs at Salzburg, Freiburg and the London School of Economics (LSE). He was joint holder of the 1974 Nobel prize for economics with Gunnar Myrdal. He also made significant contributions to constitutional law and political theory.

HDI: see *human development index*.

headline inflation: a rise in the average level of prices measured by the *retail price index* which includes the mortgage interest payments and *indirect taxes* that are excluded from other measures of *inflation*.

hire purchase: a form of consumer borrowing which is agreed at the time of purchasing the product.

■ Usually a deposit is paid and equal monthly payments are made to cover the original price plus a rate of interest on the loan.

historic cost: the original purchase price of a product or productive factor.

■ Over time *inflation* makes this number meaningless and the replacement cost can be significantly different from historic cost.

hoarding: when individuals or firms hold cash in a form that cannot be recycled through the economy.

■ Individuals holding cash in a piggy bank have withdrawn that money from circulation. If that same money had been deposited in a bank account, then it would be available as a source for borrowing. Hoarding is not usually accounted for in simple economic models, but it is important in that it can be a permanent withdrawal from the circular flow of income.

holding company: a firm that owns sufficient share capital in a number of other firms to have a controlling interest in each.

■ Often a holding company merely has a financial interest in the company and is not concerned with its day-to-day running. This means that the companies owned may have similar financial characteristics but be very different in every other respect. Therefore, many holding companies are described as conglomerates.

homogeneous product: when a firm's product is identical to that of another.

■ This is one of the main simplifying assumptions of *perfect competition*. As such it is useful but unrealistic because most firms try to make their products at least slightly different from their nearest competitors.

■ *e.g.* Currency in the foreign exchange markets and cereal crops.

horizontal integration: where firms at the same stage in the production process merge to produce one firm.

■ *e.g.* Coal mining firms at the primary stage, car manufacturers at the secondary stage, telecom companies at the tertiary stage.

hot money: a term given to large speculative flows of money that move quickly from country to country looking for the highest rate of return and speculative gains on anticipated changes in a currency's external value.

■ Because these flows are large, they can potentially destabilise domestic economies. If government is prepared to raise interest rates to a more attractive level, hot money flows could be helpful in supporting a currency that has come under pressure because of weak balance of payments numbers.

human capital: the result of investment in human resources.

■ Education, learning and training are all investments that help to make labour more productive. Many countries without significant land resources stress the importance of investment in their people and promote the idea of a knowledge-based society.

■ *TIP* It is interesting to note that in more developed countries education is often given a much lower priority than in less developed countries, where it is often seen as the single most important way that a person can raise themselves out of poverty.

human development index (HDI): a measure of the quality of life in different countries which uses a range of criteria including per capita income, life expectancy, and literacy rates.

■ It was developed by the United Nations and offers a clearer comparative measure of living standards than just *national income*.

■ *TIP* A popular examination question looks at the extent to which national income reflects living standards. The HDI is a useful attempt at combining income and other relevant criteria.

hyperinflation: a rate of *inflation* so fast that *money* loses its ability to function and people return to *barter* or use a resource which has *inherent value* or, if available, use a foreign currency.

■ After the First World War, Germany printed money in an attempt to pay its reparations. The result was that inflation accelerated between 1914–23 to a level where prices were rising by the minute and, consequently, the currency collapsed. Hyperinflation destroys contracts that have been made in money to the benefit of debtors and the cost of creditors.

■ *e.g.* From July to October 1923, German prices rose by 5,882,352,900%.

hypothesise: to reason from limited information about the effect of a change in one variable on another variable.

■ *e.g.* A monetarist might deduce that a 10% growth in the money supply, given no change in national output, raises inflation by 10% after a time-lag of 12 months. In 1 year's time empirical testing will support or refute this hypothesis.

■ *TIP* The difficulty with hypothesis testing in economics is that assumptions have to be made about many variables or the *ceteris paribus* clause needs to be invoked.

hysteresis: originally a scientific term which stated that equilibrium was dependent upon the history of the system within which it functioned. It has been adopted by economists to help explain, among other things, the natural level of unemployment.

■ Hysteresis helps explain why countries with a different history produce a different natural level of unemployment.

IBRD: see *International Bank for Reconstruction and Development.*

idle money balance: *notes* and *coins* withdrawn from the *circular flow of income* and held in the form of wealth.

■ In *Keynesian economics* these balances are held for speculating on a rise in the value of money. The expectation that *interest rates* are going to rise and *bond* prices fall means that cash will be held until the bond prices are judged to be at their lowest level when the cash will buy more interest-bearing bonds.

illiquidity: describes an asset that is difficult to turn into cash.

■ As there are degrees of liquidity and illiquidity the term is used in a relative sense. See *liquidity.*

IMF: see *International Monetary Fund.*

imperfect competition: a market with a number of competing firms, but one which does not have some or all of the characteristics of *perfect competition.*

■ There are two slightly different meanings in economics textbooks: either they include all theories of the firm that are not perfect; or they include only those theories of the firm that lie between perfect competition and *monopoly.* Given the first definition, *monopolistic competition, oligopoly* and monopoly would be examples of imperfect competition, whereas in the second definition monopoly would be excluded as there is no competition given a single-firm industry.

■ *TIP* To avoid any misunderstanding when answering a question on imperfect competition, clearly state whether monopoly is to be included or excluded from your definition.

imperfect market: this exists when any or all of the following are present: *product differentiation,* barriers to entry and exit for buyers and/or sellers, imperfect information on the price of products and/or productive factors, *collusion* between producers and/or consumers, consumers not maximising utility and producers not maximising profits.

■ In reality, all markets are to a greater or lesser degree imperfect. The concept of a perfect market is an attempt at simplification to aid comprehension.

import quota: a restriction on the physical quantity of a product imported from a foreign firm or country.

▓ Usually this is a device to protect domestic industry from competition. At the same time it has the disadvantage of restricting consumer choice.

imports: goods and services which are produced in foreign countries and consumed by people in the domestic economy.

▓ In the case of goods, national boundaries are crossed by the product, while services such as tourism may be consumed by people who cross national boundaries. In either case, the *money flow* requires domestic currency to buy foreign currency.

import substitution: a strategy often considered by developing countries as a way of promoting growth through the substitution of domestic production for imports.

▓ Politically it used to be easier to gain support for a policy of import substitution than for *export-led growth*. However, in hindsight, it seems that policies of import substitution have been less successful at raising *economic growth* than those policies that concentrated on exports.

import tariff: a *specific tax* or an *ad valorem tax* which is placed on a chosen imported product.

▓ Specific tariffs are a fixed amount per imported product, while ad valorem taxes are usually at a percentage rate, and therefore the amount of tax paid rises with the price of the import. Domestic industry receives some protection but consumers are denied choice at a lower price.

incidence of taxation: where the *tax burden* settles.

▓ A rise in an *expenditure tax* will usually produce a shared tax burden dependent upon the *elasticity of demand* for the product. If the product has a perfectly inelastic demand curve, then the consumer will pay, while with a perfectly elastic demand the producer will pay. Usually a normal downward-sloping demand curve will produce a shared incidence. At first sight, the burden of a *direct tax* like *income tax* falls entirely on the individual. However, further analysis may show that higher income tax raises wage demands and this imposes a cost that is paid for out of profits and even lost jobs.

income: payment received in money or kind by individuals or aggregated by groups as in the rewards to the *factors of production*.

▓ *e.g.* Income from employment, self-employment, welfare benefits, ownership of assets measured as wages, rent, interest, profits or aggregated to produce national income.

▓ *TIP* In answering a question on income, refer to all the rewards accrued by productive factors and not just wages.

income differential: a variation in factor reward between different people in the same country and between different people in different countries.

▓ The fact that there are considerable differences is of interest to the economist. In individual countries there are many different labour markets where supply and demand come together at significantly different levels. When comparing the income of the top 10% and the bottom 10% of a country's population, differentials are greater in the less developed countries than more developed countries.

income effect of a price change: when there is a rise or fall in the price of a product, the consumer receives a real income effect and is able to buy more or less of this and other products in spite of the fact that nominal income is unchanged.

▓ Coincidental to the income effect of a price change, there will also be a *substitution effect* from the same price change as consumer satisfaction per unit of money spent is now different.

income elasticity of demand: the responsiveness of demand for a product to a change in income.

▓ The most commonly used formula is:

$$\text{income elasticity of demand} = \frac{\%\ \text{change in quantity demanded}}{\%\ \text{change in income}}$$

There are two important aspects of income elasticity. First, if the calculation produces a positive answer, then this will describe a normal good where a rise in income raises demand for the product. A negative answer characterises an inferior good where a rise in income has led to a fall in demand. Second, the demand for luxuries will tend to have a more elastic response to a change in income, while the demand for necessities will tend to have a relatively inelastic response to changes in income.

incomes policy: an attempt by government to keep some control over wage inflation and/or levels of employment by direct or indirect action over rises in factor rewards.

▓ Some policies have been attempts to cover all labour markets; others have targeted specific areas. They have required voluntary actions or imposed compulsory limits. Monetarists criticise these policies for only exerting a short-term effect and for distorting labour markets. They assert that there is no such thing as *cost–push inflation* which renders income policies useless in fighting *inflation*. Despite considerable use during the 1960s and 1970s, the failure of incomes policies to achieve targets led to their general abandonment, although most contemporary governments of developed nations try to keep the public sector under tight control even when labour shortages seem to have been the result of depressed wages.

income tax: a payment to the Inland Revenue out of individual earnings.

▓ In the UK, income tax is the most important tax in as much as it provides the greatest proportion of tax revenue. It is progressive on taxable income after allowances, which means that as an individual's income rises, not only is more tax paid but also a larger proportion of that income is paid to the government in tax.

▓ *TIP* Mistakes are often made in calculating progressive income tax, so work through the following theoretical example where the tax rates are as follows:

Taxable income	Tax rate
0–£5,000	15%
£5,001–£10,000	20%
£10,001–£20,000	30%
Over £20,000	40%

On a £37,000 income with tax allowances of £6,000, the end-of-the-year tax liability is £9,150. This figure is arrived at as follows:

		Tax (£)	Remaining taxable income (£)
£37,000–£6,000		–	31,000
First £5,000 @ 15%	=	750	26,000
Next £5,000 @ 20%	=	1,000	21,000
Next £10,000 @ 30%	=	3,000	11,000
Remaining £11,000 @ 40%	=	4,400	0
		9,150	

increasing returns to scale: when the same proportional increase in the use of all productive factors gives rise to increasing additions to total output.

▨ *TIP* This is a *long-run* phenomenon that should not be confused with the increasing marginal returns that occur in the short run when variable *factors of production* are added to a *fixed factor*.

indexation: the process whereby nominal money contracts are adjusted in line with some measure of changes in the value of money.

▨ This nullifies the side effect of *inflation* which is a redistribution of income and wealth that has a damaging effect on anyone with nominal savings contracts and fixed income. Those most likely to be affected, and therefore protected by indexation, are the poorer and weaker members of society.

▨ *e.g.* The index linking of wage contracts or savings contracts to the *retail price index*.

index number: a chosen base number which is adjusted up or down to reflect a percentage rise or fall in a specific economic variable.

▨ The number 100 is commonly used as the base index number so that a percentage fall does not introduce the complication of a negative number. Often, after significant changes, the number is rebased to 100.

▨ *e.g.* Index numbers are used in the retail price index and indices of wages, output, exports and imports.

▨ *TIP* Because the percentage changes are added to or taken away from the previous year, a raw comparison is only easily made with the base year. Look at the following numbers:

Year 1	100
Year 2	115
Year 3	140

The percentage difference between years 1 and 3 is a rise of 40%. However, the difference between years 2 and 3 is a rise of 21.74%, i.e. $25/115 \times 100$.

indirect tax (also called 'expenditure tax'): payment to government that is levied on specified goods and services and is therefore indirect in the sense that it is only paid when the product is purchased.

▓ This tax is collected by HM Customs and Excise and usually has an incidence such that the *tax burden* is shared between producer and consumer given a normal-sloping demand curve.

▓ *e.g.* *Value added tax* and *excise duty*.

induced investment: a purchase of *capital* that directly results from of an increase in the level of *national income*.

▓ In macroeconomic models, the assumption that investment is induced means that a rise in national income causes an increase in investment. This is a basic assumption of the *accelerator theory* of investment.

▓ *TIP* Do not confuse induced investment with *autonomous investment*, which assumes that a rise or fall in investment changes national income and is therefore the basis of the *multiplier* effect of investment on national income.

industrial inertia: a situation where firms remain in a location that is no longer the optimum or most efficient site.

▓ An economic reason for this is that the cost of moving to a new site is prohibitive. The firm is therefore vulnerable to competitors who could undercut its price from a new location.

industrialisation: a reference to the development of manufacturing industry in a *developing country*.

industry: a collection of firms producing the same or similar products.

▓ Sometimes the term is used to identify all the productive activity that takes place in a certain geographical area, e.g. Scottish industry.

inelastic: where the responsiveness of demand to a change in price or income, or the responsiveness of supply to a change in price, produces, from the relevant calculation, an answer that lies between 0–1.

▓ The relevant description is that a change in the denominator, i.e. price or income, produces a less than proportionate change in quantity demanded or supplied.

infant industry: a collection of firms with a relatively immature cost structure compared with similar industries in other countries.

▓ In the early stages of development, the unit or average costs of production fall towards the lowest point on the average cost curve. If there are significant *economies of scale* and firms in other countries have reached capacity output, then the infant industry is not competitive. Arguably, an infant industry could have a comparative advantage, but it will need protection from the older established firms until it has achieved a competitive cost structure.

▓ *TIP* In theory, this provides a good economic argument for protection. In reality, it is difficult to estimate whether there is a potential for comparative advantage, and there is also a difficult decision to make regarding a right time to remove protection.

inferior product (also called 'inferior good'): a good or service with a negative *income elasticity of demand.*

▓ It can be inferred that any inferior product has a superior alternative. When the price of an inferior good changes, there is a substitution effect and an offsetting income effect. The offsetting income effect may be less than the substitution effect. In this case, the inferior product has a normal demand curve. However, if the income effect is greater than the substitution effect, as in the special case of a *Giffen good*, then it has a perverse demand curve.

inflation: a rise in the average level of prices over a measured period of time, usually stated at a yearly rate.

▓ **TIP** There is an important debate among economists over the cause of inflation. The Keynesians argue that inflation can be caused by demand–pull at *full employment* or by cost–push at less than full employment. Monetarists argue that there is only one cause of inflation at any level of economic activity, which is too much money chasing too few products. It is essential to recognise that it is not sufficient to describe inflation by rising prices, but by a rise in the average level of prices. Remember, it is possible to have some prices rising when the average level of prices falls.

inflationary gap: when the level of *aggregate demand* exceeds the *aggregate supply* at *full employment* and causes a rise in the average level of prices.

inflation tax: where the government finances its expenditure by an expansion in the money supply, and the resulting inflation reduces the value of money, thus acting as a tax on money balances.

▓ **TIP** A rise in tax caused by inflation is the only tax change that does not need to be ratified by an act of parliament. In this sense, it therefore represents an unconstitutional tax.

inherent value: this is usually a reference to types of money that also have value in use as well as exchange.

▓ **e.g.** Gold coins could be melted down and made into jewellery whereas *Bank of England* notes have no inherent value, only a value in exchange.

inheritance tax: sometimes incorporated in *capital transfer tax*, this is a wealth tax paid after a person's death on the value of their estate above an exempt limit.

injection: an exogenously determined flow into the *circular flow of income.*

▓ This is generated autonomously and, in basic economic models, includes government expenditure, investment and exports. In macroeconomic models, injections are assumed to be unrelated to changes in *national income* and their action has a *multiplier* effect on the change in national income.

innovation: the process of an *entrepreneur* bringing new ideas to the market in anticipation of a profitable return.

▓ **TIP** Innovation is separate from invention or the creation of the new idea. The term is often misused when the innovation or innovator is confused with the invention or inventor.

integrated transport policy: a focus on the way in which all of the *transport* *modes* can be linked to produce a strategy for reducing the negative *externalities* and increasing the positive benefits of moving people and freight around the country.

inter-bank market: a flow of lending and borrowing between banks and other financial institutions that allows them to adjust their short-term liquidity positions.

■ The trades are for large amounts and the money contracts are made at call and short notice as well as for relatively short fixed periods, often with firms of money brokers acting as intermediaries.

interest rate: the cost of borrowing money or the price of capital or the reward for parting with liquidity.

■ The *opportunity cost* of spending money is the rate of interest foregone by not saving the money. In terms of the productive factor capital, the rate of interest is the price paid to use money in forming capital. If the investment is financed by borrowed money, then this is an explicit cost. If the money is generated internally, then the opportunity cost is the rate of interest foregone.

■ *TIP* There are two theories of interest rate determination to consider. They are the *loanable funds theory* and the *liquidity preference theory*. It is important to understand the difference between them. Loanable funds theory analyses the market for loans, while liquidity preference analyses the market for money.

interest rate differentials: the different rates for borrowing and lending money in various parts of the market.

■ These differences may be the result of such things as: term of maturity, risk of default, expectations of future changes in rates, size of the loans, level of security backing the loan and marketability of the asset offered as security, expectations regarding inflation, expectations regarding exchange rates, interpretation of international factors, assessment of business risk and imperfect information.

■ *TIP* In an examination, read the question carefully to clarify whether it is about how the pure rate of interest is determined, or whether it is about why different rates of interest exist at any one point in time.

International Bank for Reconstruction and Development (IBRD): set up in 1945 at the *Bretton Woods* conference to allocate capital for European reconstruction projects.

■ Now more commonly known as the World Bank, its main objective is to assist the economic development of member countries with loans on reasonable terms for up to 15 years.

international debt: the money owed to a country or its private banks or to international loan agencies like the World Bank, by other countries. See *debt problem*.

international liquidity: having sufficient internationally acceptable funds to complete all necessary international trade in a multilateral trading model that uses a variety of currencies.

■ In the past, gold, acceptable strong currencies and *special drawing rights* (SDRs) raised international liquidity, while more recently, the dollarisation of many countries using currency boards, the *single European currency*, more efficient foreign exchange and eurocurrency markets, and the international credit card have all contributed to raising international liquidity.

International Monetary Fund (IMF): established in 1945, after agreements made at the *Bretton Woods* conference, to facilitate international monetary co-operation and help correct *balance of payments* disequilibrium under a *fixed exchange rate* system.

In the current world of predominantly floating rates, the IMF oversees exchange rate policies and assists countries that find their currencies under pressure. The assistance may be contingent on prescribed austerity measures.

international trade: the purchase and sale of goods, services and assets across national boundaries.

Like internal trade, which benefits from the division of labour, specialisation of function and *comparative advantage*, international trade produces the same gains, but with the added difficulty of having to trade in different currencies.

interventionist policy: a government action designed to improve the working of a *free market*.

Interventionism is supported by economists who believe government is more efficient than the market at allocating resources, particularly when there is significant *market failure*. There are degrees of intervention and almost all economists agree that it is necessary for government to become involved in the collective demand for *public goods*. Keynesian economists praise the virtue of a mixed economy where intervention is necessary to iron out fluctuations in economic activity at the macro level. Going further, socialist and Marxist economists question the principles upon which capitalism is built and, in pursuit of fairness, they argue for a *centrally planned economy* with common property rights.

inventory: a stock of unsold products and work in progress that has not reached a buyer.

Prudence requires most firms to hold stocks of products to guard against unanticipated fluctuations in demand. These inventories are usually intended, although they may be unintended when unexpected increases or decreases in demand take place and stock output ratios move outside the expected range.

investment: the process of purchasing capital assets.

In a more general sense, investment is taken to mean expenditure on things that are not for current consumption but will affect future consumption. This includes human capital and inventory building. In macroeconomic models of the economy, investment is a flow that may be induced by changes in national income or it may be an autonomous injection into the *circular flow of income*.

invisible balance: see *balance of invisibles*.

invisible hand: the unseen *market forces* that allocate resources through the *price mechanism*.

The term is usually taken to mean the opposite of government intervention.

Adam Smith, in **The Wealth of Nations**, first used the term when he wrote: 'Every individual acting solely in pursuit of private gain is led by an invisible hand to promote an end which was no part of his intention.' The 'end' is a reference to a benefit greater than that to the individual and the process assumes private property rights and freedom of contract.

▣ *TIP* An interesting point is that the invisible hand works to allocate resources at no money cost to society, whereas government intervention has to be paid for by the taxpayer.

involuntary unemployment: in Keynesian analysis this refers to people who are unemployed due to deficient *aggregate demand*.

▣ There are two interpretations of the Keynesian solution to this problem. One is that a rise in aggregate demand increases prices, lowers real wages and makes it profitable to employ more people. The other suggests that the *aggregate supply curve* is *perfectly elastic* at less than *full employment*, and therefore aggregate demand can increase employment at constant prices.

isocost line: a curve that joins together different combinations of productive factors (usually *labour* and *capital*) that cost the same to employ.

▣ The point of tangency between an isocost line and an isoquant is the least cost combination of productive factors that can produce a given output.

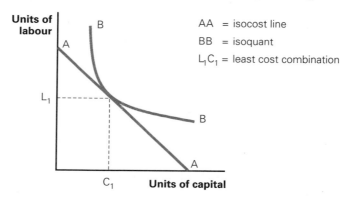

isoquant: a curve that joins together different combinations of productive factors (usually *labour* and *capital*) that can produce the same quantity.

▣ The point of tangency between an isoquant and an isocost line is the least cost combination of productive factors that can produce a given output.

issue department: part of the *Bank of England* responsible for the issue of notes and coins.

▣ Under the 1844 Bank Charter Act, the issue department was separated from the banking department. Although originally responsible for the *fiduciary issue*, the bank was allowed to print more notes when it became the repository for the country's gold reserves, but it returned to a fiduciary issue when gold joined the *foreign exchange reserves* in the *exchange equalisation account*. By 1930, the issue department accepted unsold government debt and printed notes against its security. Arguably, this caused a problem when interest rate policy and debt levels came into conflict. Monetarists have suggested that the high level of inflation during the 1970s was due to the issue department's excessive printing of cash.

■ *TIP* Monetarists consider the balance sheet of the issue department as an important indicator of future average price levels. However, Keynesians ignore these numbers because they are only accommodating more important fiscal changes in the economy.

issuing house: employed to take responsibility for the new issue of shares, debentures and bonds on behalf of firms that wish to expand their equity, or new firms going public for the first time.

■ The issuing house is often a merchant bank and it helps produce the prospectus as well as advise on amounts, timings and price for the issue. It may arrange for the issue to be underwritten and eventually dispatches the shares to their owners.

j-curve effect: the situation that occurs after a *devaluation* when an immediate worsening of a *balance of payments* current account deficit takes place before it starts to improve.

■ The reason for this is that a devaluation has the immediate effect of lowering *export* prices and raising *import* prices on the current level of sales. This leads to a widening of the gap between the value of exports and imports. After a time-lag, and dependent upon demand elasticities, the volume and value of exports increase and those of imports decrease.

■ *TIP* The graphed shape from the current balance measured on the vertical axis and time measured on the horizontal axis looks like a letter J tipping slightly to the right.

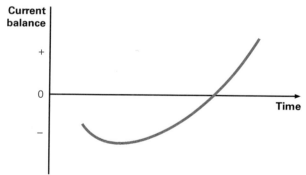

job satisfaction: the *non-pecuniary benefits* from employment in certain jobs that can add value to the pecuniary wage.

■ It may explain why a person remains in one job when the foregone alternative offers a higher nominal wage.

■ *e.g.* Reputedly, jobs like teaching and nursing attract people when offering relatively lower pay because the employee discounts job satisfaction.

jobseekers' allowance: see *unemployment benefit*.

joint demand: see *complementary products*.

joint profit maximisation: when firms agree to restrict output and raise price in collusion rather than competing with each other.

■ It is considered theoretically possible, in an oligopolistic industry, for there to be few enough firms for them to come to an agreement and stick to it. The problem that exists is that, given joint profit maximisation, each firm makes more profit than it would in a competitive situation. However, if any one firm cheats on the agreement, there is an opportunity to make even more profit as long as all the other firms are unaware of the situation and keep to the agreement.

■ *TIP* It is useful to compare the outcome from joint profit maximisation with that from *game theory.*

joint stock company: a firm whose shareholders have *limited liability* so that they only risk losing the value of their shareholding.

■ Joint stock companies were set up to encourage private ownership in a system which had predominantly unlimited liability. This meant that a person buying into a company could risk losing everything if the company went bankrupt. Private joint stock companies can have their shares owned privately, while public joint stock companies can have their shares bought and sold by any member of the public through a stock exchange.

joint supply: a situation where the process of producing one product inadvertently produces another product.

■ *e.g.* Beef and cow hide; lead and zinc; wooden furniture and saw dust.

■ *TIP* It is common to ask questions about what happens to the price and output of one product in joint supply if there is a change in the supply or demand conditions for the other product.

joint venture: when the public sector and private firms get together to provide a particular good or service.

■ This can happen in less developed countries where access to capital is limited, or it can happen in more developed countries when high capital costs, high risk or significant externalities make cooperation the most likely way to produce a particular product.

just price: derived from given social and moral criteria, this is not likely to be an economic price.

■ However, it is likely to be considered in a situation where a marketplace does not allocate resources efficiently as in the case of a *merit good*, or in a *centrally planned economy* where the state is concerned with the *national interest.*

Keynes, John Maynard (1883–1946): considered by many to be the most influential economist of the twentieth century.

▓ Keynes is recognised both for his contribution to economic theory and — often against the assumed wisdom of his day — for being at the forefront in applying much of that theory. He was a member of the Royal Commission on Indian Currency and Finance and worked at the *Treasury*, from where he represented the UK at the Paris peace conference in 1919. He was critical of the level of reparations Germany was asked to pay and did not agree on the terms for returning to the *gold standard* after the First World War. On moving to a teaching post at Cambridge University, he still played a role in formulating government policy. Keynes made significant contributions to the *Bretton Woods* conference in 1944 and was instrumental in setting up the *International Monetary Fund*. His most significant work, ***General Theory of Employment, Interest and Money***, became the handbook from which many macroeconomic models developed and much macroeconomic management was undertaken by government. Before Keynes, governments were reactive: during a slump they received less tax and spent less money; during a boom they received more tax and spent more money. After Keynes, governments became proactive by setting a target for stabilising the economy at a *full employment* equilibrium. This meant less tax and more spending during a slump, and more tax and less spending during a boom.

Keynesian consumption function: the relationship between changes in income and changes in consumption.

▓ The theory is based on the assumption that consumption is a function of current disposable income and the *marginal propensity* to consume is less than one and declines as income rises. Sometimes known as the 'absolute income hypothesis', it produces significantly different predictions to those of the *permanent income hypothesis* and the *life cycle hypothesis*.

Keynesian economics: a school of thought developed by Keynes and his followers, many of whom were and are Cambridge economists.

▓ Much of Keynes's work offered a new approach and a different insight into managing the economy. Keynesian economics offers a methodology for *fine-tuning* the overall level of economic activity at a *full employment* equilibrium.

Without economic management, the economy could settle at a less than full employment equilibrium or become overheated. The role of government is likened to that of a thermostat on a central heating system. When the economy is overheating, *aggregate demand* can be reduced using *fiscal policy* and budgeting for a surplus, whereas if the economy slows down and unemployment rises, then the government can boost aggregate demand by budgeting for a deficit.

▓ *TIP* Keynesian *demand management* seemed to be a practical success during the 1950s and 1960s, although other schools of thought were critical. The *monetarists* came to greater prominence during the 1970s when techniques of demand management seemed to be causing *inflation* alongside higher *unemployment*, and it is now rare to hear politicians talking of managing aggregate demand. At a practical level, Keynesian economics is being replaced by *supply side economics*.

kinked demand curve: at the prevailing market price, an oligopolistic firm perceives a kink in its demand curve even though the industry demand curve is a normal shape, sloping downward from left to right.

▓ Above the kink, the demand curve is relatively elastic while below the kink, it is relatively inelastic — it is the kink that provides one explanation of the motivation that oligopolists have to collude rather than compete. The kink for the firm is explained by the reaction of other firms to the individual action of one firm. If the firm raises its price, it loses customers to its competitors who keep their price at the same level and are happy to accept the increased demand. However, should the firm lower its price, it gains the potential to attract a significant number of customers away from the competition. Their reaction might be to lower their prices rather than lose customers and the only gain would come from a share of the overall increase in market demand at the lower price.

▓ *TIP* This is a good example of where a clear illustration in an examination can show understanding. In the diagram below, a rise in price, P_2, above the prevailing market price, P_1, reduces demand significantly more than the fall in price to P_3 raises demand.

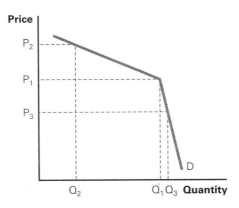

labour: one of the four *factors of production*, along with *capital, land* and *enterprise.*

■ Labour includes the mental and physical human effort used in the production of goods and services.

labour force: all persons within a given area who are working or looking for work, i.e. the employed plus the unemployed.

labour hoarding: when a firm holds on to labour during an economic downturn rather than shedding it as the profit-maximising model predicts.

■ Reasons for labour hoarding are that a firm has invested heavily in the training and development of its employees and anticipates an upturn when the labour will be required. Unskilled labour is therefore less likely to be hoarded than skilled labour. It also means that during a downturn, unemployment rises less than expected and that during an upturn, employment creation is less than expected.

labour intensive: a relative statement comparing the *capital:labour ratio* or the labour:output ratio of certain firms or various industries in the same country or throughout the world.

■ *e.g.* Agriculture in a less developed country may be described as labour intensive compared with a more developed country where it is considered capital intensive. Personal services, like hairdressing, are described as labour intensive whereas tyre manufacture is described as capital intensive.

labour market: where the interaction of supply and demand produces a *market clearing price* for a particular type of labour.

■ In any economy labour is not homogeneous and there are many different labour markets. There are only a limited number of people who have the skill and ability to become surgeons, or the physical and mental coordination for professional sport, or who are small enough to take specialist parts in films and so on.

■ *TIP* It is important to remember that labour markets produce different returns to labour and it is the interaction of supply and demand that affects the final wage. This means that high demand and high supply may produce a lower wage than low demand and even lower supply.

labour mobility: the responsiveness of the workforce to changing economic conditions that require people to work in different places and use different skills.

▓ In reality, labour is not perfectly mobile in either a lateral (geographical) or a vertical (occupational) sense. Frictions hold back labour and a significant proportion of the workforce does not regard itself as mobile in a geographical sense. Also, one unit of labour is not a perfect substitute for another and therefore a surplus of labour in the retail sector is not likely to replace a shortage of labour in the computer programming sector.

▓ *TIP* Textbooks often refer to labour immobility as a labour *market failure*. However, it should be noted that only a proportion of the workforce needs to be responsive to changing economic conditions. A rule of thumb is that the faster the rate of economic growth, the more mobile the workforce needs to be to facilitate the necessary economic change.

labour productivity: a measure of output per person which divides the physical output or the value of output of a firm by the units of labour used in the process.

▓ *TIP* The calculation of labour productivity can be somewhat misleading in that it assumes all output is determined by labour and therefore does not account for the productivity of other factors. Therefore, a company which is capital intensive shows higher labour productivity than a labour-intensive firm. In addition, an increase in labour productivity could simply be the result of replacing labour by machines.

labour theory of value: a theory stating that price differentials are dependent upon the quantity of labour used in their production.

▓ Classical economists like *Adam Smith* and *David Ricardo* called on the labour theory of value. Karl Marx took the idea further to explain the exploitation of labour under capitalism when he argued that only labour creates value and the capitalist extracts the surplus labour value by paying labour less than its true value.

labour turnover: an expression of the number of people leaving a firm as a proportion of the total number of employees. The formula is:

$$\frac{\text{employees leaving per year}}{\text{total employees}} \times 100$$

▓ Very high or very low turnover can be unhealthy. Very high turnover requires high retraining costs, time required for new employees to reach peak efficiency and concern about fundamental problems in the firm. Very low turnover may not lead to the infusion of new ideas, or the acceptance of new working practices and profitable innovations.

Laffer curve: shows a functional relationship between changes in tax rate and changes in tax revenue.

▓ Named after the contemporary American economist, Arthur Laffer, the curve identifies an optimal tax rate for income above and below which the *tax revenue* falls. Above the optimal rate, people are discouraged from additional work or hard work and may be encouraged to avoid and evade tax. In the diagram below, T_1 represents a tax rate which derives the highest tax take.

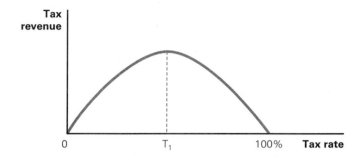

▧ *TIP* The Laffer curve is politically significant because it gives a government, which finds itself to the right of T_1, the opportunity to lower tax rates and raise tax revenue — in political jargon, a 'double whammy'.

lagged relationship: when the value of a dependent variable in the present is related to the past value of one or more independent variables.

▧ Lagged relationships are used in more complex economic models to reflect the thread of time that passes through all economic systems.

laissez faire: a doctrine that suggests society is served best through the decisions and actions of individuals rather than through centralised planning and control of the economy.

▧ Early free-market ideas were developed by the French economists François Quesnay (1694–1774) and Anne Robert Jacques Turgot (1727–81). *Adam Smith* made the point that individuals acting in their own self-interest inadvertently benefit society. Smith thought that economic welfare is maximised through the actions of individuals under a government limited to the provision of the public good. Today, the laissez-faire approach is fleshed out by the economic liberals who argue for a free-market economy, private property rights and a government that maintains a competitive framework by ruling out anti-competitive practices.

land: one of the four *factors of production*, along with *capital, labour* and *enterprise*.

▧ The factor of production that includes all the gifts of nature that are useful to people.

▧ *e.g.* Minerals, forests, lakes, the sea and all that is within it.

▧ *TIP* Remember, in economics water is land, although you should not try walking on it.

leakage: an alternative name for a withdrawal from the *circular flow of income*, the main ones being savings, taxation and imports.

▧ *TIP* Even though imports enter the economy, the income to pay for them leaks out of the country, so do not confuse the real flow and the money flow.

legal tender: any means of payment that a debtor can legally compel a creditor to accept in full and final settlement of a debt.

■ All notes (and coins up to a specified amount) issued by the *Bank of England* are legal tender in the UK. These specified amounts include up to £1 of 1ps, £5 worth of 5ps and 10ps, and £10 worth of 20ps and 50ps. The reason for this is to protect traders from the person who has saved all their 1ps in a jar and then goes to the shops to buy an expensive item.

■ *TIP* The majority of transactions by value are made using forms of *money* that are not legal tender such as *cheques* and *credit cards*.

leisure: in economic models, those hours during the day when labour chooses not to work.

lender of last resort: the responsibility of a country's *central bank* to provide liquidity to the commercial banking sector on request.

■ Commercial banks accept short-term deposits from customers who expect to be able to have their deposits returned in cash. In order to earn higher returns, a proportion of bank lending is longer-term advances to customers which are illiquid. An unexpectedly high demand for cash could leave banks short and it is at this point that the central bank can supply the necessary liquidity.

less developed country: an alternative way of describing *developing countries* that has the advantage of being a relative statement which recognises the continuing process of growth and development.

■ In this way, all countries can be compared as more or less developed rather than using the outdated absolute terminology of developed and undeveloped.

liability: a claim that individuals or groups have against them.

■ *e.g.* A financial liability to a bank is the deposits made by customers, whereas an individual's overdraft at the bank is the customer's liability.

■ *TIP* Remember that the same sum of money can be both an asset and a liability. In the example above, the customer deposit is a liability to the bank and an asset to the customer, while the overdraft is a liability to the customer and an asset to the bank.

LIBOR: see *London Interbank Offer Rate*.

life cycle hypothesis: an aggregate consumption function based upon an individual's perception of his or her lifetime income.

■ People's incomes over a lifespan can be converted into single figures to represent their annual permanent income. This is the maximum amount that can be spent on consumption each year without accumulating debts that are passed on to future generations. During the early years of adulthood, current income is below permanent income and debts increase, particularly when a mortgage is taken to buy a house. Later in life, these debts are paid back when current income is above permanent income. Therefore, given knowledge about a population's age structure and income, an aggregate consumption function can be constructed.

■ *TIP* In answering any question about the consumption function, remember this hypothesis, the *Keynesian consumption function* and the *permanent income hypothesis*.

LIFFE: see *London International Financial Futures and Options Exchange.*

limited liability: this applies to most UK firms and means that the liability of the owners of a firm is limited to the value of their shareholding.

▇ Restricting shareholders' liability encourages people to invest by limiting the risk to the amount originally invested rather than — in the event of a firm's failure — making any larger call on their personal wealth.

limit pricing: an attempt to maintain an entry barrier into an industry by setting a price just below the minimum unit cost that would be profitable for a potential new entrant.

liquidation: when a firm ceases to exist either because its assets are sold and distributed to its owners and creditors, or as the result of *bankruptcy.*

▇ The difference between bankruptcy and liquidation is that a profitable firm can be liquidated, for example, as a result of the reconstruction that takes place after a merger or acquisition.

liquidity: a relative term used to describe the ease with which an asset can be turned into *cash.*

▇ Cash is 100% liquid, whereas an asset that has only sentimental value to one person is likely to be 100% illiquid. Banks require liquidity to satisfy customer demand for cash. For this reason they hold — in addition to cash — a range of assets that can be described as very liquid. These include money lent at call and short notice, *Treasury bills* and government debt with less than a year to maturity.

liquidity preference theory: the Keynesian theory of interest rate determination using the demand for and supply of money rather than loanable funds.

▇ It assumes that the supply of money is exogenously determined by the *Bank of England,* while the demand for money is downward-sloping from left to right. It comprises active balances in the form of money held for transactions and as a precaution against unforeseeable events. Both of these are unrelated to changes in the rate of interest but do depend on changes in income. However, the third demand for money is speculative and does relate to the rate of interest, therefore giving the liquidity preference curve its slope. The equilibrium rate of interest is illustrated below at r_1.

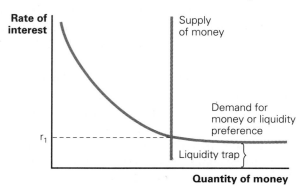

TIP When asked a question about the determination of interest rates, include both this theory and the *loanable funds theory*.

liquidity trap: the Keynesian *liquidity preference theory* states that as the money supply curve shifts to the right, so interest rates fall to a point beyond which they cannot go any lower and therefore *idle money balances* increase.

The liquidity trap occurs when people judge that interest rates have reached their lowest point and therefore hold on to speculative balances in anticipation of a rise in rates and a fall in bond prices. This means that any further attempt to lower interest rates and boost investment is ineffective.

living standard: see *standard of living*.

load factor: in transport economics, the relationship between seats available and seats taken in the various *transport modes*.

e.g. The load factor of cars driving into London is often as low as 20% when there is one driver and five seats, whereas trains during rush hour are often full or — arguably — overfull. The load factor of an airplane is very significant as high fixed costs and low variable costs mean that cheap seats may be available close to the flight time.

loan: a temporary transfer of funds from a lender to a borrower.

The borrower pays an interest charge while the lender receives interest as a reward for parting with liquidity. The rate of interest may vary as the result of the term to maturity and the assessment of risk.

loanable funds theory: an alternative theory of interest rate determination using the demand for and the supply of loans rather than the demand for and the supply of money.

According to this theory, the rate of interest is determined by the supply and demand for loanable funds in financial markets. The supply of funds comes from people's decision to save, while the demand for loans includes funds for investment and other forms of borrowing such as hire purchase and mortgages. If people are supplying funds to the market that cannot be lent on, the interest rate falls to attract borrowing and discourage saving. Also, if the demand for loans increases, the rate rises to encourage more saving and discourage borrowing.

TIP When asked a question about the determination of interest rates, include both this theory and the *liquidity preference theory*.

local labour markets: these exist because of the uneven distribution of population and the frictions imposed by the cost and time of travel.

The same labour market may be subdivided across the country, producing income differentials at the local market clearing rate.

location theory: attempts to explain why firms and industries are located in particular places.

The analysis of location by economists often involves two distinct elements. First, the optimum location for a firm choosing a new location and, second, the reason why firms exist in their current location. The latter involves a historical perspective to explain how times may have changed to leave a formerly well-placed firm operating some distance from a current optimum location.

▨ *e.g.* Steel-making firms were originally located near coal mines, but when the coal was used up they would have been more effectively located near the coast to take advantage of imported coal.

London Interbank Offer Rate (LIBOR): a variable base rate of interest paid on loans made in various currencies, maturing on different dates and for different amounts through the eurocurrency market.

London International Financial Futures and Options Exchange (LIFFE): pronounced 'life', this is where traders and speculators guarantee future prices for buying and selling a range of sterling and foreign currency assets.

long run: that period of time which allows all the *factors of production* to change, although technology is held constant.

▨ The time period referred to is particular to each industry. It may take years before a firm producing electricity can build a new power station, whereas a firm that is developing new computer software may only take a day to change all its productive factors.

long-run average cost curve: a line plotted from the calculation that divides the total costs of production by the number of units produced when all the *factors of production* are variable.

▨ The normal long-run average cost curve has a U-shape which is determined by the economies and diseconomies of large-scale production. Inside the curve are many overlapping short-run average cost curves which are tangent to the long-run curve as illustrated in the diagram below.

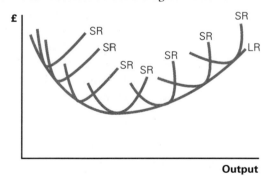

▨ *TIP* Points of tangency have the same slope, so only at the lowest point on the long-run curve is the corresponding short-run curve at its lowest point.

long-run marginal cost curve: plots the additional cost of producing one more unit against output given that all the *factors of production* are variable.

▨ Its shape is determined by the *long-run average cost curve*. If this is U-shaped, the marginal curve starts by falling faster than the average curve, turns upwards through the lowest point on the average curve and then continues to rise at a faster rate.

Lorenz curve: a visual representation of income inequality achieved by plotting the cumulative percentage of total income received against the cumulative percentage of total population.

■ An equal distribution of income produces a 45° line. The greater the divergence from this line, the greater the inequality represented by the Lorenz curve. In the diagram below, the ratio of the area enclosed by the line of equality and the Lorenz curve and the total area under the line of equality is known as the Gini coefficient.

■ *e.g.* If the shaded area in the diagram is 8 units and the area of the triangle BCD is 32 units, then the Gini coefficient is 0.25. Absolute equality produces a coefficient of zero while absolute inequality is unity.

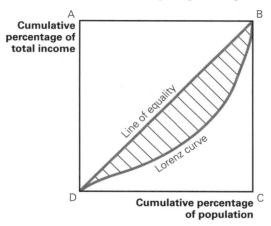

loss leading: when a firm chooses a product from its range to sell at a unit loss anticipating that customers will be attracted to buy its more profitable products.

■ *e.g.* Supermarkets place loss leaders near the entrance and then require the customer to walk down many aisles before reaching the exit. Computer software firms may sell their programs at a loss towards the end of their life, hoping to attract buyers to their new version.

loss minimisation: the assumed motivation of a firm in the *short run* when it is making a loss but can still, at least, cover its variable costs.

■ Loss minimisation and profit maximisation both occur when the firm produces where marginal cost equals marginal revenue when marginal cost is rising.

luxury: the name somewhat crudely given to products which have an *income elasticity of demand* which is elastic (greater than one).

■ It means that a rise in income causes an even greater percentage increase in demand and therefore an increased proportion of income is spent on the product. Products with an income elasticity of less than one are commonly referred to as *necessities*.

Maastricht Treaty: signed in December 1991 by member states of the *European Union* to agree the introduction of a single currency along with agreement for combined policy action covering industry, welfare, foreign policy and defence.

▨ The UK negotiated an opt-out clause for the single currency with a possible entry option at a later date.

macroeconomics: the study of economics at the level of the national and international economy.

▨ Macroeconomics is concerned with the theory and practice of the *circular flow of income*, the management of the economy, economic problems such as *inflation, unemployment*, low growth and *balance of payments disequilibrium*, and the relationship between one economy and another in an international setting.

▨ *TIP* In the past, there was a clear division between macroeconomics and micro-economics, but more recently, the lessons learnt on one side are being considered relevant to the other side. *Keynesian* demand side management of the economy was a macroeconomic policy, whereas management through supply side policies is very much at the level of microeconomics.

Malthus, Thomas Robert (1766–1834): a clergyman and academic best remembered for his *An Essay on the Principle of Population* which suggested that populations grow geometrically (2, 4, 8, 16), while the ability to feed them grows arithmetically (2, 4, 6, 8).

▨ Malthus provided a scientific explanation for the crises of malnutrition, plagues and wars that act as checks on population growth. In the more developed world, the slowing of population growth rates and the increased intensity of food production have relegated his ideas to academia. However, in the less developed world — where population growth is faster and the growth of agri-cultural output is slower — wars and famines are still prevalent. There are environmental economists who invoke Malthusian ideas to predict that unfettered population growth and competitive *economic growth* will cause the world to use up its *non-renewable resources* and suffer a steep decline in living standards.

managed float: a floating currency where market forces are the main determinant of the exchange rate, but where it is well known that government is prepared to intervene in exceptional circumstances.

■ A market intervention where government actions are not signalled is described as a *dirty float*.

margin: the point at which the last unit of a product is consumed or produced.

marginal cost: the additional cost of producing one more unit of a product, although reference can be made to the marginal cost of producing additional units, i.e. another five or ten units.

■ Bearing in mind that fixed costs do not change with output, so marginal cost is determined by the variable costs of production. Occasionally, the marginal cost refers to the last unit produced, in which case it is written as $TC^n - TC^{n-1}$, i.e. the total cost of producing a certain number of units minus the total costs of producing one less unit.

marginal cost pricing: equating the price of the product with the marginal cost of producing the last unit.

■ This gives rise to *allocative efficiency* and is considered as one possible pricing policy for products produced in the government sector. In theory, marginal cost pricing occurs under perfect competition in either the short run or the long run as p = mc and mc = mr: the profit-maximising rule. However, under *imperfect competition*, including *monopoly*, p > mc where mc = mr and therefore allocative efficiency cannot be achieved if the profit-maximising rule is followed.

marginal efficiency of capital (also called 'marginal efficiency of investment'): the additional output produced by the last unit of capital employed.

■ A profit-maximising firm uses units of capital up to the point where the additional revenue received from the last unit of capital employed is equal to the rate of interest (price of capital).

marginal factor cost: the extra cost of employing one more unit of a given productive factor.

■ Alongside *marginal revenue product* it is used in a labour market to illustrate simple wage theory.

marginal physical product: the additional output produced by a firm when one more factor of production is added to the production process.

■ It is usually applied to labour but could be used to convey information regarding any productive factor.

■ *TIP* In the final analysis, marginal physical product is far less important to the employer than the revenue to be gained from the sale of the physical product. Therefore, it is usual to convert the above into the value of the marginal physical product or *marginal revenue product*.

marginal private benefit: the addition to total satisfaction felt by an individual when one more unit of a product is consumed.

■ It does not include any external benefit that may be felt by society and can be represented by the price a person is willing to pay to buy a product.

marginal private cost: the addition to total cost of producing one more product.

■ It does not include any external costs that may be felt by society and is easily measured from a firm's accounts.

marginal propensity: the extent to which a dependent variable changes as the result of a change in an independent variable.

▓ *e.g.* marginal propensity to consume (c), import (m), save (s), tax (t), withdraw (w), is calculated using the formula:

$$\text{marginal propensity to c, m, s, t, w} = \frac{\text{change in c, m, s, t, w}}{\text{change in income}}$$

▓ The answer shows the proportion of an increase in income that will be consumed, imported, saved, taxed or withdrawn.

marginal rate of substitution: the additional quantity of one product or productive factor required to replace another product or productive factor to maintain the same outcome for the consumer or producer.

▓ In the case of a producer, it is how much capital is required to substitute for the loss of a unit of labour to maintain the same output. For the consumer, it is how much of one product is required to substitute for the loss of another to maintain the same level of satisfaction.

marginal rate of tax: the tax paid on incremental amounts of a taxable quantity such as income, wealth or expenditure.

▓ It is commonly referred to when analysing the progressive nature of *income tax*. In the past, marginal rates have risen as high as 98% of each addition to income. This was an 83% rate on all earned income above a certain level and a 15% supplement on unearned income. See *Laffer curve*.

▓ *TIP* The calculation of tax taken from progressively higher marginal rates of taxation is often miscalculated. See *income tax*.

marginal rate of transformation: a measure of the slope of the *production possibility curve* that shows how much production of one product is lost by producing more of the other product.

▓ It is the same as the ratio of the marginal cost of producing one product to the marginal cost of producing the other product.

marginal revenue: additional revenue received from the sale of one more product.

▓ If the demand curve is perfectly elastic (as in *perfect competition*), then marginal revenue is equal to price. However, under *imperfect competition*, the downward-sloping demand curve means that marginal revenue is less than price. This is because price has to be lowered for all products in order to sell one more product.

marginal revenue product: the marginal physical product of a *factor of production* multiplied by the *marginal revenue* from the sale of the additional units of output.

▓ In the case of *perfect competition*, it is marginal physical product multiplied by the price of the product, whereas for imperfect competition, it is marginal physical product multiplied by marginal revenue from the sale of the additional units of output.

marginal revenue product curve: a line that joins together all the points that record the value of the additional output produced by employing one more factor of production.

■ The curve is usually applied to labour. *Division of labour* and specialisation of function mean there are normally increasing additions to total revenue product before diminishing marginal returns cause the curve to turn down. The marginal revenue product curve below the average revenue product curve is the demand curve for labour given the assumptions of one variable factor, a perfectly elastic product demand and profit maximisation. In the diagram below, point A is where the demand curve for labour starts. At any wage rate above point A it is not profitable to employ anyone. Below point A, returns to employing labour are maximised as illustrated by W_1Q_1, W_2Q_2, W_3Q_3, or any point along the marginal revenue product curve.

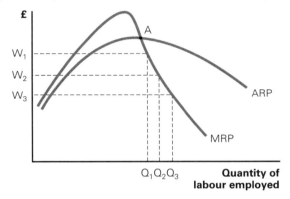

marginal revenue productivity theory of wages: states that employers hire labour up to the point where the *marginal cost* of employing labour is equal to the *marginal revenue product*.

■ If there is a perfectly elastic supply of labour, then the marginal cost of employing labour is the wage rate and the amount of labour employed is determined by the marginal revenue product curve.

■ *TIP* Criticism can be levelled against this theory in as much as it is a theory of demand for labour rather than a theory of wages. To be a theory of wages, the interaction of supply of labour and demand for labour has to be analysed.

marginal social benefit: the addition to total benefit felt by society when one more unit of a product is consumed.

■ The calculation includes the marginal private benefit felt by the individual plus any additional external benefits felt by society.

■ *e.g.* A vaccination against cholera provides a private benefit to the person involved and an external benefit to other people who cannot become infected through that person.

■ *TIP* It is a common error to assume that social benefits are the same as external benefits. They are not, because social benefits comprise private benefits plus external benefits.

marginal social cost: the addition to total costs felt by society when one more unit of a product is produced.

■ The calculation includes the marginal private cost paid by the firm and any additional external costs felt by society.

■ *e.g.* The marginal private cost of producing an additional car is paid for by the firm, but the external costs to society that may result from road congestion or additional exhaust fumes are not accounted for, but do make up the marginal social cost.

■ *TIP* It is a common error to assume that social costs are the same as external costs. They are not, because social costs comprise private costs plus external costs.

marginal utility: the additional utility derived from the consumption of an extra unit of any product.

■ In practice, it is not possible to measure utility in a meaningful way that allows comparison between people. However, it is possible to assume diminishing marginal utility on successive units of the same product for the same person, as well as to record a rank order of products for the same person.

market: where buyers communicate with sellers to exchange products.

■ The marketplace does not have to exist in physical space as trade may take place on the phone or the Internet.

market clearing price: the equilibrium price at which quantity demanded by consumers is equal to the quantity supplied by producers and the market is cleared given a specific period of time.

market demand curve: the horizontal sum of all the individual demand curves for a particular product.

■ *TIP* Horizontal sum means adding up all the quantities on the horizontal axis for each individual and plotting the aggregate totals against the market price.

market failure: the inability of the marketplace to clear products or productive factors efficiently.

■ There are degrees of market failure. In the case of *public goods* there is almost total failure as the non-rival, non-excludable characteristics mean that consumer demand is missing from the equation. *Merit goods, demerit goods* and some *private goods* have significant *externalities* that do not produce an efficient allocation of resources. *Monopolies* and *monopsonies* in product and productive factor markets — along with minor market imperfections like imperfect knowledge — are mild forms of market failure.

■ *TIP* Questions on general or specific types of market failure, and how they can be corrected, are common in examinations.

market forces: the pressures which act to cause movements along and shifts in the demand and supply functions and therefore induce changes in the price and/or quantity exchanged.

market imperfection: a term used to describe events which bring about an inefficient allocation of resources in product and productive factor markets.

■ In general, market imperfection is used to describe less serious events, while *market failure* is used to describe the more serious events that disturb and distort markets.

■ *e.g.* Cartel, tied retail outlets, labour market frictions.

marketing: the activities of a firm concerned with selling and distributing its product.

■ *e.g.* Market research, advertising, transport.

marketing board: an intermediary that brings together a number of sellers and markets their products collectively.

■ Boards exist for some agricultural products to establish a stable market in terms of price and give the opportunity to farmers to market on a scale that could not be afforded by individuals. Marketing boards can only be set up where products are homogeneous as individual producers will not be identifiable.

■ *e.g.* Eggs, milk, tea, coffee, cocoa.

market separation: the market is broken down into self-contained segments and the firm can profit maximise by *price discrimination*.

■ As long as there is no seepage between the market subdivisions and conditions of demand, then different prices produce more profit than a single price. Perfect market separation absorbs the *consumer surplus* as each customer pays an individual price.

■ *e.g.* Car sales in different countries, electricity sold to domestic or industrial customers.

market share: the proportion of the market sales, in terms of volume or value, held by one firm.

■ Firms which have more than a 25% market share in the UK are assumed to have *monopoly* power and are therefore liable to investigation.

■ *TIP* Remember that, in theory, a firm is not a monopoly until it holds a 100% share of a market. However, firms in the UK and US are investigated as monopolies when they are only of oligopolistic proportions.

market supply curve: the horizontal sum of all the individual firms' supply curves for a particular product.

■ *TIP* Horizontal sum means adding up all the quantities on the horizontal axis for each firm and plotting the aggregate total against the market price.

Marshall, Alfred (1842–1924): a Cambridge economics professor who laid the foundations of microeconomic theory with contributions to consumer theory, elasticity, price determination, market equilibrium and the different time periods within which firms can respond to changed market conditions.

Marshall–Lerner condition: for a *devaluation* to be successful in improving the current account of the balance of payments, the sum of the demand elasticities for imports and exports must be greater than one (unity).

■ If the sum adds up to one, then there will be the same percentage change in the value of imports and exports.

■ *e.g.* A UK devaluation of 3%.

Price elasticity	Price change	Change in demand	Change in revenue
	EXPORTS		
0.25	Domestic output prices unchanged in terms of sterling, 3% depreciated in foreign currency	+0.75%	+0.75%
	IMPORTS		
0.75	Import prices rise by 3% in terms of sterling	−2.25%	+0.75%

The above example produces no change in the current balance if the total values of imports and exports are the same. However, if imports are greater than exports, then the same percentage change worsens the balance.

■ *TIP* Note that both price elasticities can be inelastic, i.e. less than one, as long as the sum adds up to more than one. Therefore 0.5 + 0.6 is sufficient to improve the current balance. It is a common mistake to write that both numbers must be greater than one.

medium of exchange: the main function of modern money.

■ Trust in cash, credit cards and so on means a seller is willing to accept a form of money in exchange for a product, knowing full well the medium of exchange has no *value in use* but can be passed on to someone else in exchange for a different product. In the past. assets like gold and silver, which had a value in use, also had a value in exchange because they were generally acceptable and therefore could fulfil the function of being an exchange medium.

menu cost of inflation: a reference to the fact that rising prices cause a need for menus in restaurants to be reprinted, price tags in shops to be changed and petrol price signs to be reset.

merchant bank: a *commercial bank* that specialises in business customers rather than private individuals.

■ These banks developed internationally, often specialising in particular areas of the world where they became the main vehicle for accepting (guaranteeing) commercial *bills of exchange*. Today, they have diversified into foreign exchange dealers, business advisers, experts on mergers and acquisitions, and issuing houses for stock exchanges and small unlisted capital markets. Many have been taken over and are part of large banking conglomerates.

merger: the legal joining of two firms after the owners of each firm agree to combine their shareholding to form a single new firm.

■ *e.g.* Vodafone and Airtouch, Cadbury and Schweppes, BP and Amoco.

merit good: a product which has rival and excludable characteristics but, when left to a free market, is likely to be under-consumed.

■ This is because individuals may not be aware of the intrinsic benefits of the product to themselves and neither do they account for the external benefits to society of their consumption.

▦ *e.g.* Health and education.

▦ *TIP* Remember that *merit goods* are *private goods* and not *public goods*. As governments often provide merit goods free at the point of consumption, students make the mistake of referring to them as public goods. Even worse is when merit goods are referred to mistakenly as *free goods*.

microeconomics: the study of the behaviour of small economic units such as the individual, household and firm.

▦ The small economic units are analysed in detail while *ceteris paribus* ('all other things being equal') is applied to the rest of the economy on the assumption that its relative neglect does not lead to serious errors. This form of economic investigation is known as partial equilibrium analysis while general equilibrium analysis comes under the umbrella of *macroeconomics*.

Mill, John Stuart (1806–73): an economist and philosopher who built on the work of the early classical economists by applying a more rigorous analysis of market forces and price determination.

▦ Despite his *laissez faire* tendencies, Mill recognised a role for government in the provision of law and order, social justice and education, or what today might be called the provision of *public goods* and *merit goods*.

minimum efficient scale: the scale of output of a firm that produces the lowest average cost of production in the long run.

▦ This need not be one unique point as many firms, particularly large firms, are likely to have flat bottoms to their average cost curves. The points of minimum efficient scale vary considerably between firms and this helps explain why some industries comprise many small firms while others include a few large firms.

minimum lending rate (MLR): the rate at which the *Bank of England* rediscounted first class bills for the money market when it was fulfilling its function as *lender of last resort.*

▦ Today, the MLR is not central to monetary policy and is rarely used in conjunction with the function of lender of last resort. A wider range of smoothing actions to maintain liquidity in the financial sector is taken by the Bank of England, including adjustments to the short-term rate of interest and open market operations.

minimum wage legislation: a floor below which wages cannot legally fall.

▦ In some countries, the minimum has been established with reference to an hourly rate while others have set a minimum rate for an agreed working week. The British government set the lowest legal level of payment in 1998 with an hourly rate of £3.60 which applies to all workers over the age of 21. Minimum wage legislation is an interesting area for economic analysis because the predictions from traditional theory suggest it does not have the desired effect of raising living standards at the bottom of the income scale. If the rate is set below the lowest currently being paid in any labour market, it has no effect and is a waste of administrative resources. If it is set above the equilibrium being paid in the lowest labour markets, it distorts those markets by producing an involuntary group of unemployed people as illustrated in the diagram below between Q_1 and Q_2.

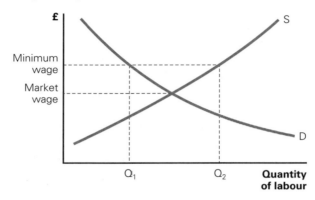

People paid at or just above the minimum wage may push for a restoration of differentials. By this analysis, the trade-off is between higher rates of pay for those who remain in employment and higher unemployment for others.

mixed economy: a combination of *free markets* and government intervention to allocate resources.

▨ Ideally, the mixed economy eliminates the disadvantages and maintains the advantages of the market economy and the *centrally planned economy*.

▨ *TIP* In reality, all countries — whatever they may call themselves — are a mixture of markets and government intervention. The interesting point is how close economic systems come to the extremes, and in which direction they are moving.

MLR: see *minimum lending rate.*

MNC: see *multinational corporation.*

monetarism: *Milton Friedman* defined it as a consistent, though not precise, relationship between the rate of change in the money supply and the rate of change of nominal national income.

▨ It is important to recognise that there is a variable time-lag between the change in *money supply* and the change in *national income*. From this relationship comes the monetarists' main prediction that *inflation* is always and everywhere a monetary phenomenon, where prices rise in response to too much money chasing too few products.

▨ *TIP* Strictly, monetarism is no more than is stated above, although other views are often included under the umbrella of monetarism, namely the promotion of free-market capitalism and a limited role for government in the allocation of scarce resources.

monetarists: those economists, including *Irving Fisher, Milton Friedman* and *Friedrich Hayek*, who accept the tenets of monetarism.

- Although they have similar views on markets and capitalism, it is not the case that all monetarists express the same view of economics, particularly at the interface with politics. Friedman pointed out that by strict definition Karl Marx and Chairman Mao were monetarists; they were certainly not supporters of free-market capitalism.

monetary base: in a modern economy the notes and coins which act as a base to the credit component of the *money supply*.

- During the era of the gold standard, gold was the monetary base upon which credit was created. Because there seems to be a consistent relationship between cash and credit measured by the bank credit multiplier, monetary base policies are an alternative way of controlling the money supply that does not require political adjustments to interest rates.

monetary policy: the way in which *interest rates* and *money supply* are used to manage the overall level of economic activity and achieve the government targets for *unemployment, inflation, economic growth* and *balance of payments*.

- The importance of monetary policy has varied from an accommodating policy that supports the fiscal targets established by Keynesian economists, to setting the monetary framework which imposes limits on fiscal decisions and creates the stable economy supported by monetarists.

Monetary Policy Committee (MPC): established along with the *Bank of England's* independence in 1997 to oversee monetary policy with particular emphasis on the interest rate and an inflation target.

- The members of the committee are independent experts who meet monthly and may agree a change to the Bank of England base rate (repo rate). The governor is chairman and the minutes are published 6 weeks after the meeting. The minutes are a source of interest as they show how the committee voted on whether or not to change *bank rate*. Trends can be estimated from the balance of votes and how they are changing.

monetary theory: looks at the role of *money* and *interest rates* in the economy, and variations that occur depending on the economic philosophy underpinning their use.

- Keynesians say money is a relatively unimportant reactive variable in the economy and argue for it being given a minor accommodating role. *Monetarists* highlight the amount of damage that can be done to an economy through monetary mismanagement and suggest that the optimum quantity of money is that which grows in line with real output. This allows more transactions to take place at the existing average level of prices and translates into a policy of establishing targets for monetary growth slightly above the expected rates of growth in output. The principle here is that a little inflation harms an economy less than a little deflation.

monetisation of debt: when government debt is bought back using printed money.

- This increases the money supply and may be the result of an overriding priority to fix interest rates at a level that does not allow money growth to get out of control.

money: an early definition of money was 'that which passes freely from hand to hand in full payment for goods, in final discharge of indebtedness, being accepted equally without reference to the character or credit of the person tendering it, and without the intention on the part of the person receiving it to consume, enjoy or otherwise use it than by passing it on sooner or later in exchange'.

■ Early forms of money, like gold, had both characteristics of *value in use* and *value in exchange*. However, modern money is a token that only has *value in exchange*. The four main functions of money are as a medium of exchange, a store of value, a unit of account and as a standard of deferred payment. The main characteristics of modern money are that it is generally acceptable, divisible, portable, relatively scarce, durable and stable in supply over long periods of time. The demand for money is usually divided into transactions, precautionary and speculative.

■ *TIP* When answering a question on money, do not confuse functions and characteristics.

money at call: a loan from a *commercial bank* to the *discount market* that can be recalled immediately if the banks find themselves short of *liquidity*.

■ It is therefore a very liquid asset and because of the risk to the discount house, the negotiated rate of interest is relatively low. The bank, however, earns interest on an asset which it would not otherwise receive if held as cash.

money at short notice: lent by a *commercial bank* to a variety of institutions on terms that usually range from overnight to 7 days.

■ The asset is very liquid but not quite as liquid as money at call.

money balance: money held for transactionary, precautionary or speculative reasons in the form of cash or in chequeable accounts.

money flow: recognition that units of money are used more than once in the process of trade.

■ The result of this is that any measured income over a specific period of time is greater than the economy's stock of money.

■ *e.g.* If income is 30 and money supply is 10 then, on average, each unit of money will have been used three times over the period that generated said income. See *velocity of circulation*.

money illusion: when people respond to changes in the nominal value of money irrespective of what has happened to the real value of money.

■ *e.g.* People may refer to a wage rise when a nominal increase of 5% occurs alongside an inflation rate of 10%. In fact, they should refer to a fall in wages. Keynes pointed out that workers were less likely to respond negatively if the nominal wage rose even if the real wage fell, than if the nominal wage fell irrespective of what happened to the real wage.

money market: in its narrowest sense, refers to the London money market where discount houses borrow money at call and short notice from the commercial banks at low rates of interest in order to buy mainly discounted trade and *Treasury bills* of exchange.

■ In a wider sense, the money market refers to a number of different markets that deal in short-term loans and deposits, including the inter-bank market and the market for sterling certificates of deposit.

money multiplier: see *bank credit multiplier.*

money supply: a measure of the total quantity of *money* in an economy at any one point in time.

■ It is difficult to measure precisely, which is why there are a range of monetary measurements. Some of them understate the amount of money in the economy, i.e. M0, and others overstate the amount of money, i.e. M4, which includes near money in the form of savings accounts. M0 is a narrow measure of money that includes notes and coins in circulation plus banks' till money and balances held at the *Bank of England*, and probably accounts for less than 10% of the transactions that take place by value on any one day. M4 is a broader measure of money that includes notes and coins in circulation, private sector chequeable accounts, private sector bank deposits and holdings of money market instruments such as *Treasury bills*.

■ *TIP* M0 and M4 are the two most commonly referred to measures of the money supply, but the measure that probably comes closest to a true measure of money supply is M1, which includes notes and coins in circulation and private sector current accounts and deposit accounts that can be transferred by cheque.

monopolies, mergers and restrictive practices acts: a series of acts in the UK since the Second World War designed to promote competition and outlaw activities that create excessive producer power.

■ Today, firms which control more than 25% of the market or, through mergers, may be considered to have monopoly power or, through agreed restrictive practices may be limiting fair competition, are liable to investigation.

■ *TIP* In the UK, these forms of investigation may or may not lead to legal action. This pragmatic approach is different from the US approach where firms breaking anti-trust laws are liable to prosecution without question, e.g. Microsoft.

monopolistic competition: a competitive industry where there are a large number of firms producing products which are similar but differentiated, usually by a brand image, and where there is free entry into and exit from the industry.

■ *Product differentiation* means that each firm faces a *demand curve* that slopes downward from left to right. The less differentiated the product, the more elastic is the demand curve; the more differentiated the product, the less elastic is the demand curve. The profit-maximising equilibrium for the firm in the short run can be the same as the monopoly diagram. However, free entry into the industry means that new firms are attracted by excessive profits and reduce market share for the existing firms. This produces a long-run equilibrium where the firm makes *normal profit* as illustrated in the diagram below at P_1Q_1.

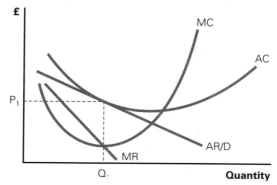

■ *TIP* This is one of the main theories of the firm and it is necessary to study it in some detail. To avoid a common mistake when drawing the above diagram, proceed in the following order: draw AC, MC, AR; mark on P_1Q_1; draw MR so that it cuts MC above Q_1. Sometimes students are confused when they see the terms monopoly and competition in the same description. Remember, competition comes from many firms producing similar products and monopoly refers to the product differentation caused by such things as the name and brand image.

monopoly: in theory, this is a single firm industry where one producer has control over the supply of the product and can maintain control in the long run.

■ In reality, any firm with more than a 25% share of a market is described as having monopoly power and is liable to be investigated. The monopolist is a price-maker by description, but has no power to influence demand. However, the monopolist is aware of the nature of demand and can offer that quantity to the market that yields the largest profit. *Barriers to entry* into the industry produce a long-run profit-maximising equilibrium at P_1Q_1, with excessive

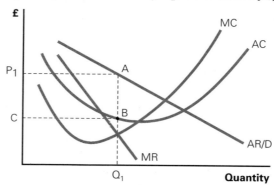

profits being the rectangle between AC and AR at P_1ABC. This is illustrated in the diagram above.

TIP The diagram that represents long-run equilibrium for the monopolist can also be used to illustrate a short-run equilibrium under *monopolistic competition*.

monopoly power: when one firm is large enough to dominate a market or several firms collude to influence price or output, and therefore increase their collective profits.

■ Degrees of monopoly power are recognised from the true monopoly in a single firm industry through oligopolies and even, to a lesser degree, in the product differentiation that exists under monopolistic competition.

■ *e.g.* Heinz (baked beans) and Guinness present a powerful image in their industry and therefore maintain a degree of monopoly power.

monopoly profit: the name given to the *excessive profit* that can be sustained in the long run by a monopolist as *barriers to entry* stop new firms entering the industry.

monopsony: a single buyer of a product or *factor of production*.

■ The term is most commonly used in labour markets where a one-firm town could be the sole buyer of labour in a particular area, or the government could be the sole buyer of civil servants. A monopsony buyer in a labour market faced with a competitive supply of labour can force the wage below the free market equilibrium. It is less common to use the term in product markets, but degrees of monopsony power exist where large retail outlets, like Marks and Spencer, buy all the output of a small clothing firm.

■ *e.g.* The beginnings of a monopsony are being established on the Internet where a firm takes orders from customers and then goes to the supplier to organise a group discount which is shared between the Internet firm and the customers.

mortgage: a type of loan usually made to purchase property where the debtor secures the loan by allowing the creditor (bank or building society) to be the owner or part owner of the property until the creditor is repaid, when ownership reverts to the original debtor.

movements and shifts: a movement along a supply or demand curve means that more or less is being supplied or demanded as the result of a change in price, and should not be confused with a shift, where more or less is supplied or demanded at the same price.

MPC: see *Monetary Policy Committee*.

multilateral trade: where more than two countries trade without any requirement for bilateral reciprocity.

■ For all countries, the flows of trade are in balance, but this need not be the case between pairs of countries. Germany could be in deficit with Japan but in surplus with America. In a multi-currency trading system, a *foreign exchange market* is the main facilitator of multilateral trade.

multinational corporation (MNC): an international *firm* based in one country but with wholly-owned and partly-owned subsidiaries in other countries.

■ In addition to *economies of scale*, multinationals take advantage of tax and subsidy variations between countries and are on a strong footing in any negotiations with government.

■ *e.g.* Shell, Microsoft, Toyota, Coca-Cola.

multiplier: the number of times that an injection into or withdrawal from the *circular flow of income* raises or lowers total income.

■ The symbol K represents the multiplier and it can be calculated from the change in income (ΔY) and the change in the injection (ΔJ) or withdrawal (ΔW). It is written as:

$$K = \frac{\Delta Y}{\Delta J \text{ or } W}$$

The algebraic formulation in a one-sector model is:

$$K = \frac{1}{1 - mpc} \quad \text{or} \quad \frac{1}{mps}$$

In a two-sector closed economy model it is:

$$K = \frac{1}{mps + mpt}$$

In a three-sector open economy model it is:

$$K = \frac{1}{mps + mpt + mpm}$$

where mpc, mps, mpt and mpm denote the marginal propensity to consume, save, tax and import respectively. The multiplier is a Keynesian concept that assumes fixed prices and therefore a change in real income. A *monetarist* interpretation with variable prices might see the change in income as *nominal, real* or shared between a change in prices and a change in output.

NAIRU: see *non-accelerating inflation rate of unemployment*.

national debt: the sum total of debt accumulated by central government.

■ National debt came into existence along with the establishment of the *Bank of England* in 1694 by William III, by the end of whose reign the debt was £49 million. In recent years, the debt has fluctuated at around one third of *gross domestic product*. It can be divided into marketable debt, which can be traded on securities markets, and non-marketable debt, such as national savings. The term can be used to cover all public-sector debt, including the debt of local authorities and nationalised industries.

■ *TIP* Although the trend has been for the nominal national debt to rise, the real national debt has fallen during those years in which the *inflation* rate grew faster than the debt. *Monetarists* point out that governments can overspend their budgets, finance the deficits by printing money, cause inflation and yet still lower the real value of national debt.

national income (also called 'net national income'): the total sum of all incomes earned in the economy over 1 year, adjusted for depreciation (*capital consumption*).

■ There are three measures of national income which, after adjustment, produce the same total. They are: adding up all the incomes from wages, profits, interest and rent; adding up the value of the output of all firms in the country; and adding up the spending of consumers, government and industry, adjusted for international trade. Despite the errors and omissions inherent in gathering such a large quantity of data, the national income accounts provide useful time-series data on the changing state of the economy. It is common to measure national income *at market price* or *at factor cost*. Also, a measure at constant price is used to identify changes in real output.

national insurance: the tax paid by employers, employees and the self-employed to provide a basic structure of welfare support that includes payments during illness, pensions, child and maternity benefits and unemployment benefits.

national interest: a normative term often used to describe government actions in the economy for which there is no clearly measurable outcome.

■ It may be judged that policies to redistribute income and wealth, to nationalise certain industries, to protect producers from foreign competition and to protect consumers from exploitation by monopolies are all in the national interest.

nationalised industry: private firms transferred into the public sector of the economy, where they continue trading under state ownership and control.

■ The process of nationalisation started under the Labour government (1945–51) and involved much of the country's heavy industry. The Conservative government (1979–97) reversed the process with a policy of denationalisation which began with the privatisation of British Telecom.

■ *TIP* All nationalised industries are public corporations, but not all public corporations are nationalised industries, e.g. the Forestry Commission and the BBC. Nationalised industries should not be confused with the National Health Service or state education, which are departments of government. British industry which has remained nationalised includes the Post Office and Civil Aviation Authority.

national minimum wage: see *minimum wage legislation*.

natural monopoly: when a single firm has gained control of an industry without that being its target.

■ If a firm actively tries to create monopoly status for itself, then it is referred to as a contrived monopoly. Natural monopolies develop mainly when one firm or business has sufficient technical *economies of scale* to satisfy all the market demand more efficiently than two or more firms. This means that the demand curve intersects the firm's average cost curve when it is still falling or at its lowest point. Other types of natural monopoly can result from the uneven concentration of natural resources. There is a tendency towards monopoly power when certain products — champagne, for example — rely upon crops, which can only be grown in certain regions.

■ *TIP* Although natural monopoly is 'of nature' in the case of a concentration of natural resources, it is important to remember that natural monopoly can occur in other situations which have not been contrived.

near money: liquid assets that are very close to being used as *money* but require a small change before they can fulfil the main function of money as a *medium of exchange*.

■ *e.g.* Deposit accounts at banks and savings accounts in building societies which have to be turned into cash or shifted into a chequeable account before they can be used to buy goods and services.

■ *TIP* Confusion results from the fact that some broad *money supply* aggregates, like M4, include a significant proportion of near money. In the past, near money changed into money when building societies offered cheque books with certain of their savings accounts. The government's prime money supply target grew rapidly, without a change in the country's stock of money, when banks started to offer mortgages and potential homebuyers shifted their funds from building societies, which were outside M3, to banks which were inside this monetary aggregate.

necessity: a product with an *income elasticity of demand* that is relatively inelastic, which means that consumer demand changes less in percentage terms than the change in income.

▨ *e.g.* Bread, milk and heat.

need: different from demand, in that need is judged by the fact that certain products, like *merit goods*, are needed more than they are demanded and therefore, in a free market, they are under-consumed.

▨ *e.g.* Education and health care.

negative externality: a third-party effect from either production or consumption that imposes a cost on society which is not paid for by the producer or consumer.

▨ *e.g.* A negative externality (external cost) of production is a discharge of waste into the local river that damages the ecosystem. A negative externality (external cost) of consumption is lung cancer caused by passive smoking.

negative income tax (also called 'reverse income tax'): a proposed tax system which would replace the benefits system by paying a tax credit for every pound not earned below the tax threshold.

▨ A unified system of negative income tax would remove the *poverty trap*, in which attempts by low income earners to increase their earnings causes them to lose entitlement to benefits and to pay tax: a person might earn an additional pound and lose more than one pound in tax and benefits. Under a negative income tax system, many more unemployed people would be prepared to take part-time jobs, as no one could be worse off.

▨ *e.g.* Suppose a person starts to pay income tax at 30% after the threshold of £6,000 and a negative income tax is set at 40%. This means that for each pound not earned below £6,000 a person receives 40p. The table below shows that a person can never be worse off, no matter how little additional income they earn.

Income (£)	Tax paid (£)	Tax credit received (£)	Disposable income (£)
0	0	2,400	2,400
1,000	0	2,000	3,000
2,000	0	1,600	3,600
3,000	0	1,200	4,200
4,000	0	800	4,800
5,000	0	400	5,400
6,000	0	0	6,000
7,000	300	0	6,700
8,000	600	0	7,400
9,000	900	0	8,100
10,000	1,200	0	8,800

neighbourhood effect: the term given to *externalities* that have a localised effect.

■ Although often used as a synonym for externalities, the neighbourhood effect refers to localised external costs rather than benefits. This excludes an external cost like exhaust fumes and their effect on global warming.

■ *e.g.* Smoke from factories, heavy lorries on local roads, noise pollution.

net advantage: in wage theory this is the movement to equalise advantage as people transfer out of less desirable jobs and search for more desirable jobs, therefore causing a rise in wages for less desirable jobs and a fall in wages for more desirable jobs.

■ When *pecuniary rewards* and *non-pecuniary benefits* are taken into account, there is an equalisation between labour markets. However, this assumes that labour is homogeneous and perfectly mobile. In reality, there are frictions that hold back movements between labour markets, and differences in relative skills and abilities that create static equilibrium differential rewards that do not change over time. We cannot all be steeplejacks or brain surgeons.

net investment: gross investment minus the investment necessary to replace capital consumed in the production process.

■ Net investment says more about the state of an economy than gross investment (see *gross domestic fixed capital formation*). If net investment is negative, society is not replacing all the capital consumed in production and is therefore likely to suffer a reduction in future output and a negative effect on living standards. If net investment is positive, there is likely to be a rise in future output and a positive effect on living standards.

net national income: see *national income*.

net property income from abroad: the difference between income from assets held abroad and income paid to foreigners holding assets in a given country.

■ In the more developed countries, this figure is usually positive, while it is usually negative in the less developed countries.

new issue market: the primary market of the long-term capital market, dealing with the issue and underwriting of new shares.

■ The issue of new shares is a way of raising long-term finance for a firm. It gives more flexibility in the distribution of profits than does the commitment to make regular interest payments and final repayment of loans. The primary market includes issuing houses and insurance underwriters.

■ *TIP* It is a common error to refer to the stock exchange as the institution that deals with new issues. In fact, the stock exchange only deals in second-hand securities.

newly industrialising country (NIC): a *developing country* that has moved on from a reliance on *primary industry* to the development of *secondary* and *tertiary industry* and the creation of an economic and social infrastructure.

■ *e.g.* Brazil, Korea, Malaysia.

NIC: see *newly industrialised country*.

NIMBY: see *not in my back yard*.

nominal: a measurement in terms of money which, when applied to changes in income, may or may not reflect *real* changes.

▓ *e.g.* Nominal wages rise by 5%, but, if there is 10% inflation, then the real value of wages falls.

non-accelerating inflation rate of unemployment (NAIRU): a level of *unemployment* that cannot be reduced in the long term by increasing *aggregate demand*.

▓ The only difference between NAIRU and the natural rate of unemployment is that NAIRU assumes an *inflation* rate that is constant, while the natural rate of unemployment assumes stable prices. Where an economy has a NAIRU that is considered too high, the only way to reduce it is through *supply-side* policies.

▓ *TIP* NAIRU or the natural rate is often assumed in models developed by non-Keynesian economists. The terminology is commonly associated with the work of the monetarist economist *Milton Friedman*. In contrast, Keynesian economists stress full employment and under-full employment equilibriums and do not accept the NAIRU concept.

non-diminishable product: see *non-rival product*.

non-excludability: characteristic of a product which, when offered to any one person, also becomes available to all other people.

▓ There is a collective demand for the product but no individual demand as people are not prepared to purchase a product if they cannot exclude other people from benefiting. See *free rider*.

▓ *e.g.* A *public good*, such as defence or street lighting, has non-excludability.

non-pecuniary benefit: a non-money benefit that can be enjoyed in certain types of employment.

▓ Job satisfaction can be considered to be part of the reward to the productive factor, labour. Often jobs which help people have non-pecuniary benefits.

▓ *e.g.* It is generally accepted that many teachers and nurses accept lower salaries than they could earn in alternative jobs because of the non-pecuniary benefits of job satisfaction.

non-price competition: a situation in which firms have agreed or have been forced to compete in ways other than through price.

▓ This is often an assumed characteristic of *oligopoly*, where firms are reluctant to change price when they are faced with a *kinked demand curve*. Non-price competition may involve, for instance, heavy advertising budgets, free gifts at the point of sale, special promotions and exclusive packaging.

non-renewable resource: a resource which is finite in supply and, once consumed, cannot be replaced.

▓ These resources are of particular concern to gloom-and-doom economists who foresee that a competitive race to use up these resources will eventually lead to a fall in living standards. A contradictory view suggests that the *price mechanism* will ensure that they are not used up. When their price rises to a level that makes them uneconomic in their current use, they will be replaced by cheaper, natural or synthetic resources.

▣ *e.g.* Coal, oil, natural gas, mercury, aluminium.

non-rival product (also called 'non-diminishable product'): a product which, when consumed by any one person, is still available to others in equal quantity.

▣ Products with this characteristic are usually *public goods* that cannot be allocated through a price mechanism, but require financing through taxes or licences.

▣ *e.g.* A radio signal picked up by one person does not reduce its availability to other people.

normal good: see *normal product.*

normal product (also called 'normal good')**:** a product for which a rise in price leads to a fall in quantity demanded (and vice versa), while a rise in income leads to a rise in quantity demanded (and vice versa).

▣ Another way of saying this is that when people get richer they buy more of a normal good. All *luxury* products are in this category and those that are not normal — which is when demand rises when consumers become poorer — are *inferior products.*

▣ *TIP* A normal product has the two characteristics described above, but an *inferior product* has only one characteristic, which is a perverse relationship to changes in income. An inferior product can have a normal or a perverse demand curve, as in the case of a *Giffen good.*

normal profit: the minimum reward an *entrepreneur* requires to remain in a particular line of business.

▣ Normal profit is the *transfer earning* of the entrepreneur. If the profit falls below this level, the entrepreneur transfers resources to another business. In economics, normal profit is considered to be the cost of *enterprise* and only *excessive profit* is looked at as a surplus reward or *economic rent.*

normative economics: based upon *value judgements* rather than positive statements.

▣ A normative statement is often prefaced by 'ought to be' or 'should have been'. Arguably, normative economics takes over where positive economics finishes.

▣ *e.g.* Statements about the *national interest* are often based upon value judgements, for example 'monopolies ought to be regulated', 'aggregate demand should not have been expanded' or 'pensions must have been mis-sold'.

notes: the paper form of *money* which was originally receipts for assets, usually gold, held at goldsmiths and banks.

▣ *Bank of England* notes still have printed on them 'I promise to pay the bearer on demand the sum of ...'. However, the promise is no longer honoured in terms of gold as all modern notes are token money.

not in my back yard (NIMBY): the selfishness where everyone agrees that a new motorway or prison needs to be built, but not near to where they live.

▣ The result of this attitude is that such developments are often built in poorer areas where residents are unable to set up the necessary pressure group or gain the media coverage and access to legislators required to fight a proposal.

obsolescence: a fall in the value of current capital assets resulting from the introduction of a more efficient machine or process for doing the same thing.

A value for the *depreciation of capital* takes into account both deterioration through use and obsolescence. Of the two, obsolescence is the more difficult to value as inventions and innovations are usually unexpected. A machine can become obsolescent when it is new and has never been used.

e.g. The fast rate of change in computer technology can create obsolescence in a machine that shows no signs of deterioration.

occupational mobility (also called 'vertical mobility'): the extent to which labour is able to adapt and move between occupations.

As skills become redundant, labour ideally retrains to develop the new skills required by a growing economy. There are two types of friction that restrict occupational mobility: first, labour is not homogeneous and only a limited number of people have certain skills; second, the age effect works perversely in the sense that labour is less likely to retrain efficiently at the time in life when it is most likely to need retraining. See *frictional unemployment*.

OECD: see *Organisation for Economic Cooperation and Development*.

Office of Fair Trading (OFT): coordinates the government policy aimed at promoting free and fair competition and deals with violations under monopoly, merger and restrictive practices legislation. See *Competition Commission*.

OFT: see *Office of Fair Trading*.

oligopolistic behaviour: when the few firms comprising an industry act together for mutual advantage.

Among other things, oligopolistic behaviour may involve agreements on pricing, output, market separation and advertising. Some of these actions may contravene legislation designed to promote competition.

oligopoly: *imperfect market* structure consisting of an industry made up of a few large firms which may collude to mutual advantage (see *joint profit maximisation*) or which may be forced to compete away excessive profits (see *game theory*).

There is no universally recognised oligopoly diagram as there is for the other main theories of the firm. However, there is some agreement that each firm in the industry faces a demand curve which it perceives as kinked at the prevailing market price (see *kinked demand curve*).

■ *e.g.* BP Amoco and Shell in oil, Glaxo Wellcome and Astrazenea in pharmaceuticals, Vodafone and BT in telecommunications.

oligopsony: a situation in which there are few powerful buyers in a particular market.

■ *e.g.* Some of the large retail chains — Tesco, Sainsbury's and Marks and Spencer — have significant buying power and can force down prices among the manufacturers who supply them.

OPEC: see *Organisation of Petroleum-Exporting Countries.*

open economy: an economy in which international trade exists or is assumed to exist for the purpose of constructing *macroeconomic* models.

■ Some countries have tried to remain self-sufficient and closed to the outside world, as China did under Chairman Mao. Models can be constructed on the assumption that the economy is either closed or open to international trade.

■ *e.g.* An open-economy model of the *circular flow of income* includes exports as an injection into the flow and imports as a withdrawal from the flow.

open market operations: the purchase and sale of government securities on the stock exchange by the *Bank of England* in pursuit of its *monetary policy.*

■ In the past, the buying back of government securities returned cash to the system and expanded the *money supply*. This process was reversed in order to take cash out of the system and contract the money supply. Since 1981, the emphasis of monetary management has changed and buying or selling is almost entirely limited to short-term bills, which are bought and sold on a daily basis to achieve a particular interest rate rather than directly to expand or contract the money supply.

opportunity cost: a measure of the alternative foregone when a product is produced or consumed.

■ Opportunity cost is an important concept in economics because it is a *real* measure of how scarce resources are used. It removes any misunderstanding that may result from *money illusion,* as it tells the producer that when resources are used to make this product other things cannot be produced. In the same way, the consumer is informed that the cost of buying one product is being unable to buy another. Opportunity cost analysis is particularly useful in explaining the theory of *comparative advantage.*

Type of product	Opportunity cost of production	Opportunity cost of consumption
Free good	No	No
Public good	Yes	No
Merit good	Yes	No
Club good	Yes	No
Private good	Yes	Yes

TIP It is important to separate production from the opportunity cost of consumption. The table on p. 106 clarifies whether there is an opportunity cost of production and/or consumption for different types of products.

optimum: the best situation given limiting and limited criteria.

In economics, a limited number of situations produces a best case which is referred to as optimum, while other situations produce a best case that is not an optimum. If best for the group contradicts best for the individual, then best for the group is the optimum. If several bests coincide, as they do under *perfect competition*, that position is known as optimum optimorum, that is, best of the best or, in modern jargon, 'simply the best'.

optimum allocation of resources: when a firm produces at a level of output that equates price with *marginal cost*. See also *allocative efficiency*.

optimum capacity: when a firm produces at a level of output that equates *marginal cost* with *average cost*, that is the lowest unit or average cost of production. See *productive efficiency*.

optimum level of pollution: the level at which the additional cost or damage to society from pollution is equal to the cost of removing the pollution.

In environmental economics, this is the optimum level for society of an external cost of production or consumption.

TIP Remember that the optimum level of pollution is a positive number and not zero.

optimum quantity of money: the quantity of money which changes at the same rate as changes in the *real* economy, so that all transactions can take place without putting any pressure on the average level of prices to change.

The uncertainty over the future rate of change of output in the real economy means that the ideal situation described above is unlikely to be realised. The realistic suggestion is that the *money supply* should grow at a slightly faster rate than the expected rate of growth of *output*. This is because mild *inflation* is judged less harmful to the economy than mild *deflation*.

ordinary share: an equity shareholding in the ownership of a *joint stock company* that entitles the holder to a share of the profits in the form of a *dividend*, after the debenture holders and preference shareholders have been paid.

Ordinary shareholders take more risk than preference shareholders as the return on ordinary shares is variable and may be nothing for 1 or more years. On the other hand, the return may be very high, with a corresponding gain in the asset value of the shares.

Organisation for Economic Cooperation and Development (OECD): the international association of developed countries that encourages economic growth and financial stability among its members, promotes multilateral free trade and arranges aid to *developing countries*.

The OECD was established in 1961 and offers an important educational resource, with regular reports on member countries, details of developing countries and various aid packages.

Organisation of Petroleum-Exporting Countries (OPEC): founded in 1960 to control the oil output of member countries and therefore influence world oil prices.

▓ The effect of OPEC was not felt until the 1970s, when a concerted effort to restrict supply and raise oil prices produced a significant increase in oil revenues. Once supply was controlled, the inelastic demand for oil meant that a rise in price turned relatively insignificant less developed countries into rich and powerful countries almost overnight. However, OPEC has not been able to maintain its power as, over time, non-member countries have discovered oil and the more developed world has reduced demand and dependence on oil products.

output: the finished product made by using the *factors of production* and offered in the form of either a good or a service.

▓ Output need not necessarily be for use by a consumer. The output of a component manufacturer is for further use in the production of a good or service in final demand. Output can be measured in terms of a physical quantity or in terms of its value.

▓ *TIP* The value of output can change as prices change, even though the physical quantity remains unchanged.

overdraft: facility granted by a bank to a customer to spend more money than the customer has in his or her current account.

▓ Overspending on an overdraft incurs interest charges for as long as the account remains in deficit. This facility gives customers more flexibility in their spending and allows them to smooth out any mismatch between income and expenditure.

overfunding: selling more government debt than is required in any given year to cover the *public sector borrowing requirement.*

▓ A government may use overfunding to slow money supply growth or to put downward pressure on aggregate monetary demand without imposing the same pressure on its expenditure.

overnight money: funds lent to the *money market,* usually with the expectation of repayment the following day.

overvalued currency: when a *fixed exchange rate* is higher than the free market rate and therefore foreign exchange reserves or foreign currency loans are being used to buy the currency and maintain its overvaluation.

▓ In a fixed exchange rate system, a persistent current account deficit on the balance of payments is usually symptomatic of an overvalued currency. In a floating exchange rate system, an overvalued currency is less likely to persist, although it is possible for a country to maintain the currency at an overvalued level by using a high interest rate policy. Such a policy attracts the foreign currency to purchase assets on capital account that is required to compensate for the current account deficit.

paradox of thrift: an apparent contradiction between the benefits of saving and the potential consequences of that saving.

■ An individual is encouraged to part with *liquidity* in the present in order to raise income in the future through the rate of interest paid on the saving. Saving is a withdrawal from the *circular flow of income*. Therefore, if everyone increases their saving, *ceteris paribus*, the level of national income will fall and therefore not allow for a realisation of the individual expectation of a rise in income.

■ *TIP* If the ceteris paribus assumption that all else remains equal is removed, an increase in saving is likely to lead to a fall in interest rates and a boost to investment which, in turn, will raise national income as expected.

paradox of value: a curiosity that challenged the minds of early economists, namely: why did products essential to human welfare have a low value — like water — while products which are not essential — like diamonds — have a high value?

■ The solution came from looking at relative scarcity and the difference between total utility and *marginal utility*. Water is less scarce than diamonds and if we suppose it is available free, then people consume it up to the point where marginal utility is zero and total utility is high. Diamonds are scarcer and command a price that leads to people consuming less, up to a point where they have high marginal utility but a low total utility.

■ *TIP* To fix this point in mind, ask the following question: if a person was dying of thirst and was given the choice of having the world's biggest diamond or a life-saving glass of water, which would that person choose?

Pareto optimum (also called 'Pareto efficiency'): exists when it is not possible to reallocate resources and products to make anyone better off without making someone else worse off.

■ The optimum situation described above requires both an optimum allocation of resources to production and an optimum allocation of products to consumers.

partial equilibrium analysis: the study of individual markets at the level of *microeconomics* which involves the assumption that outside the market in question, all other things remain unchanged.

This *ceteris paribus* assumption makes the analysis manageable but also introduces the possibility of error. Studies on the scale of the economy as a whole are described as general equilibrium analysis.

partnership: the next stage on from the *sole proprietor* where two or more people form a business which usually has unlimited liability such that each partner is responsible for the debts and tax liability of the other partners.

e.g. Groups of professionals in accountancy, law and medicine.

TIP Most partnerships run under the 1890 Partnership Act, which is one of the oldest surviving pieces of legislation. A Limited Partnership Act was set up in 1907, but few *firms* have taken advantage because, if *limited liability* is being considered, it is preferable to form a private limited company.

par value: either the agreed rate of exchange in a *fixed exchange rate* system or the coupon price of a financial security or the nominal price of an ordinary share.

In each of the above cases, the market price may be different from the par value.

patent: the granting of an exclusive right to an inventor to control the production of a product for up to 20 years.

The Patents Office has to be convinced that the product has original features and the controller of patents reserves the right to grant a right of manufacture to other persons if the patent is being abused.

pecuniary reward: a reward or benefit paid in the form of money.

It is possible that a person's wage can be made up of a pecuniary reward and *non-pecuniary* reward in the form of job satisfaction.

pendulum arbitration: where the arbiter of a dispute must decide in favour of one side or the other and is not allowed to offer a compromise.

Wage negotiations in Japan have had their successful outcome credited to the fact that pendulum arbitration awaits any unresolved dispute. In the UK, trade unions invariably ask for wage increases above where they expect the final rate to settle, while employers go below. If pendulum arbitration was adopted, neither side in negotiations would risk going too high or too low. Therefore, agreements are invariably made without resorting to arbitration: at least, that is how it works in Japan.

pension: a payment made to people as income after they have retired from work.

State pensions are payable to men and women after the state retirement age, while company pensions may or may not be on offer. Pensions are usually financed in one of two ways. First, those reaching retirement age can have their pensions financed by those who remain in employment. Alternatively, they can be financed from a pot of investments built up during the working lifetime.

TIP Notice that in *national income* statistics, pensions are referred to as transfer payments and excluded from the total. This is correct if they are financed by current employees but, arguably, incorrect if they are financed from a pot of financial assets.

per capita: Latin for 'by the head', this commonly appears in official data when a measure per person is required.

■ **e.g.** GNP per capita, output per capita.

perfect competition: a theory of profit-maximising firms built on the foundation of a number of unrealistic but simplifying assumptions: homogeneous product; many buyers and sellers; perfect knowledge among producers and consumers; perfect factor mobility in the long run; freedom of entry to and exit from the industry; and no transport costs.

■ Given these assumptions, the industry will be made up of many identical firms who accept the market price and therefore face a perfectly elastic demand curve. In the long run, they are allocatively efficient (P = MC) and productively efficient (MC = AC) as well as making normal profits as illustrated in the diagram below.

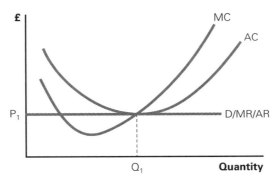

■ **e.g.** There are no good examples of a *perfect market* with perfect competition, although the *foreign exchange market* comes close with a *homogeneous product* (currency), many buyers and sellers, a good level of knowledge, reasonable factor mobility, limited freedom to enter and leave, and hardly any transport costs.

■ **TIP** Perfect competition is often criticised because it is not realistic. However, this misses the point because it is a deliberately over-simplified model designed to produce a basic level of understanding from which to build knowledge and move closer to interpreting the complexities of the real world.

perfectly elastic demand/supply curve: a line parallel to the horizontal quantity axis as illustrated below.

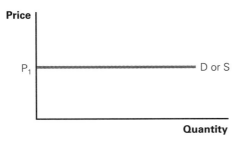

■ The difference between the curves is that at price P_1 and below, consumer demand is infinite. Above P_1, demand is zero. In contrast, producer supply is infinite at P_1 and above, and zero below P_1.

perfectly inelastic demand/supply curve: a line parallel to the vertical axis which means that any change in price will not affect the quantity supplied or demanded as illustrated below at Q_1.

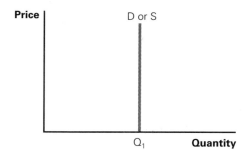

■ *TIP* Although it is unrealistic to think of a perfectly inelastic demand curve except over a limited price range, it is possible for the supply of unique items — like the painting of a deceased artist — to be perfectly inelastic in supply.

perfect market: this is sometimes considered to be synonymous with *perfect competition*, although a more rigorous description includes the requirement to have perfectly competitive firms interacting with perfectly informed, utility-maximising, competitive, mobile consumers.

permanent income hypothesis: developed by *Milton Friedman*, this assumes that people have a perception of their permanent income that determines their pattern of consumption.

■ Further to this, their actual income can deviate from their perception of permanent income without having any effect on their actual consumption. This means that changes in income that are considered temporary will have no effect on consumption. Only when they are considered as part of permanent income will they change consumption. This produces two consumption functions: a short-run function, which has little or no response to a change in income; and a long-run function, which shows more response if the change is considered permanent.

■ *TIP* The significant difference between this theory and the Keynesian consumption function is seen in their predictions of future spending. If the government reduced income tax, then Keynesians would predict an immediate change in consumption, whereas the permanent income hypothesis would estimate no change until the increase is perceived as being part of permanent income. See *life cycle hypothesis* and *Keynesian consumption function*.

Phillips curve: established from empirical observation by A.W. Phillips of the relationship between the rate of change of money wages and the unemployment rate, such that lower levels of unemployment were associated with rising wages and higher levels of unemployment with falling wages.

▨ The observations were taken over a period from 1861–1957 and the regularity of the curve suggested it could be used effectively as a predictive model. Based on the assumption that wage rises are a major cause of inflation (a point not accepted by monetarists), the Phillips curve was interpreted by some as the relationship between rising inflation and more jobs or falling inflation and more unemployment. The predictive ability of the model was brought into question in the 1970s when inflation and rising unemployment occurred together. See *augmented Phillips curve*.

Pigovian tax: named after Arthur Cecil Pigou (1877–1959) who observed that the divergence between private and social costs required an *indirect tax* to produce an *optimum allocation of resources*.

▨ Ideally, the Pigovian tax is equal to the external cost and therefore has the effect of internalising the *externality*.

▨ **TIP** In practice, it is difficult to measure precisely the external cost.

planned economy: at the extreme, this refers to a *centrally planned economy* which acts as a command economy.

▨ Alternatively, the term may be used to refer to an economy with a significant amount of government planning over the allocation of resources, but not necessarily the same degree of control.

▨ **e.g.** China's is a planned command economy, whereas Japan's is an economy where the government planned a significant role for markets.

▨ **TIP** After the Second World War, the UK economy went through a period when many national bodies were set up to advise and act on national economic plans. Over recent years, there has been a movement away from economic planning towards deregulation, privatisation and liberalisation.

PLC: see *public joint stock company*.

point elasticity of demand: an elasticity value for every point along a demand function that can be calculated by measuring the straight line distance (by a tangent if the line is not straight) from the point in question to the horizontal axis and dividing it by the distance to the vertical axis.

▨ **e.g.**

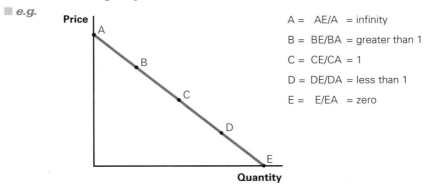

A = AE/A = infinity
B = BE/BA = greater than 1
C = CE/CA = 1
D = DE/DA = less than 1
E = E/EA = zero

TIP This is a good way of beginning to understand elasticity. It involves a simple calculation using a ruler and confirms that every point along a straight line has a different elasticity. In the case of a rectangular hyperbola, a tangent from every point along the line proves that each point is equidistant from both axes and therefore has a uniform value of one (unity).

pollution: a by-product of any activity involved in the production and/or consumption of a product that offends the senses and reduces economic welfare.

e.g. Loud noise from an airport, a coal tip that pollutes the view, atmospheric pollution that produces a bad smell, river pollution that kills the fish, sea pollution that makes it dangerous to bathe.

pollution rights: the process which sells the right to pollute in any given environment as a way of controlling and reducing pollution.

A responsible body decides on how many pollution permits are sold in a certain area. For the firm that buys them, pollution is now paid for and is therefore no longer an *externality*. When the firm judges the permit to be more expensive than installing the necessary equipment, then it acts to stop the pollution. If a local community or conservationist group wished to stop or reduce pollution, then they could buy up some or all of the permits.

positive economics: incorporates a scientific approach to the subject by going through the process of collecting facts (induction) and then deducing theories and developing verifiable hypotheses.

Much of positive economics is concerned with constructing models to predict future events with a high degree of probability. This approach to the subject does not involve *value judgement* and the opinion which is included in the realm of *normative economics*.

potential entry: the expected entry of a *firm* into an industry may be a sufficient enough threat to force firms already in the industry to keep their prices down.

Theories of the firm assume actual entry is required to reduce excessive profits, whereas, in reality, the threat of potential entry is sufficient to keep prices down in a *contestable market*.

poverty: as an absolute this is when a person does not have access to sufficient resources to sustain a healthy life; in a relative sense, poverty exists when a person's *standard of living* is below a certain specified level, usually measured in terms of *per capita* income.

Poverty is identified in more developed countries at a much higher standard of living than in less developed countries, where it is likely to be closer to absolute.

poverty trap: an overlap between the point at which a person starts to pay tax and the level at which that person receives welfare benefits.

The result of the poverty trap is that when a person works to earn more money, he or she is liable to lose entitlements to welfare payments and will have to pay tax. In the past, this has resulted in people losing more than £1 for each additional pound earned. Not only this, but there is likely to be a range over which the same person will be faced with losing 90p in the pound, 80p in the pound and so on. This leads to the perverse situation where people caught in the poverty trap lose more entitlement to income when they earn more money than the richest, highest taxed people. To clear the poverty trap, a person would have to receive a sudden large increase in income that is probably unlikely. This situation leads to a continuing dependency on welfare benefits and creates an incentive to work without declaring income.

■ *TIP* Look at *negative income tax* as a possible solution.

precautionary demand for money: when people hold *money* surplus to the requirement for transactions in case an unforeseen event requires them to make an unexpected payment.

■ *e.g.* Almost everyone reading this definition is carrying more money than they currently require to complete the day's expected transactions.

predatory pricing: where a company reduces its price to a loss-making level in order to force a competitor out of the market.

■ This usually happens when a large firm can subsidise losses in one sector from profits made in other parts of the business, while it forces a small competitor out of the market. This is difficult to prove but there are many suspicious pricing policies.

■ *e.g.* Airline ticket prices, retail electrical goods, computer software and hardware.

■ *TIP* Across national boundaries, this may be referred to as *dumping*.

preference: where a consumer states — or shows by purchase — a preference for one product over another.

■ When such a preference is expressed, it is possible to deduce that more utility is gained from the higher order ranking product and less from the lower ranking product.

preference share: one which bestows ownership rights upon the holder, who takes less of the risk of the business by usually being paid a fixed rate *dividend* out of the profits before the ordinary shareholder receives a variable dividend.

■ Preference shareholders rank below *debenture* holders who receive interest on their loan even if the firm does not make a profit, whereas the preference shareholder is the first claim on profit.

price: the nominal value given to an economic item which is traded between two parties.

■ The price may vary during a process of negotiation between both parties from the original price at which the item was offered for sale. Also, the price may be adjusted over time as the result of changes in the conditions of supply and/or demand.

price discrimination: see *discriminatory pricing* and *market separation*.

price elasticity of demand: a measure of the responsiveness of quantity demanded to a change in price.

■ Where point elasticity produces a value for each point along a demand curve, price elasticity produces a calculation between points, or over the arc of the curve, and is therefore an average of points or a percentage change from one point to another. The most common formula is:

$$\text{price elasticity of demand} = \frac{\text{\% change in quantity demand}}{\text{\% change in price}}$$

Although it is often ignored, a minus sign in front of the equation is strictly necessary to produce a positive answer.

■ *TIP* There is an important relationship between elasticity, sales and revenue. If the demand curve is elastic, a fall in price raises demand and revenue. If the curve is inelastic, a fall in price raises demand and reduces revenue. A straight line demand curve illustrates this point well and is commonly misinterpreted by students who make the mistake of assuming a rise in quantity demanded also raises revenue to the firm. The diagram below shows how total revenue rises as price falls over the elastic range and falls as price falls over the inelastic range.

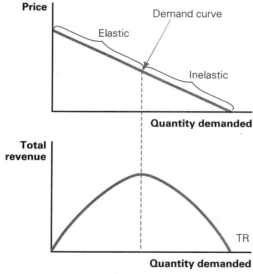

price elasticity of supply: see *elasticity of supply.*

price maker: a term used to describe the ability a monopolist has to set a price rather than accept the market price, as occurs under *perfect competition.*

■ *TIP* It is a common error to assume that the monopolist can control both price and output. This is not correct — it is consumers who determine market demand. Therefore, if the monopolist makes a price change, output is determined by the market.

price mechanism: a reference to the way changes in relative prices act as market signals to producers to allocate resources in response to consumer demand.

■ Given only two competitive products, X and Y, suppose demand for X rises and demand for Y falls. The price of Y falls and a new profit-maximising equilibrium is at a lower level of output. This releases resources to be used in the production of X whose price has risen to a new profit-maximising equilibrium at a higher level of output. In reality, this mechanism is distorted and disrupted by market imperfections and *market failure*. However, in many cases, the simplified description above is a close approximation of what is happening in a market economy. Also, the price mechanism works best when changes in the average level of prices are kept to a minimum, preferably zero. This allows the signalling mechanism of relative prices to work at its best.

price taker: a term used to describe the way in which a perfectly competitive firm has no influence over price and has to accept the given market price.

■ The perfectly competitive firm can only adjust output to achieve a profit-maximising position. As each firm has such a small share of the total market, the demand curve for the firm is perfectly elastic. This means that individually, no one firm can change output sufficiently to affect price.

primary industry: a collection of firms that extract the raw materials from nature that are used in the manufacture of goods (*secondary industry*) and the provision of services (*tertiary industry*).

■ *e.g.* Agriculture, forestry, fishing, mining and quarrying.

private benefit: the satisfaction received by an individual from the consumption of a product which is not passed on in the form of any external benefit to society.

■ Usually the expected private benefit from a product is reflected in the price a consumer pays for the product.

private cost: a cost incurred by the firm when it produces a product, excluding any external costs, that may be passed on to society in the process of production, distribution and selling.

■ Usually the private costs can be read from the firm's profit and loss account.

private enterprise: where firms are owned by individuals, partners or shareholders, and any proceeds from successful business, usually in the form of profits, are available for distribution to those owners of the enterprise.

private good: a product which has the characteristics of being *rival* and *excludable*.

■ *e.g.* Food and clothing.

private property rights: a situation where individuals or groups can take over legal ownership of property and exclude other people from using or benefiting from this property.

■ Some economists consider this the fundamental right upon which *capitalism* is founded and the driving force behind the engine of *economic growth*.

privatisation (also called 'denationalisation'): the transfer of state-owned industry back to the private sector of the economy — usually through the sell-off of shares — which turns the industry into a *public joint stock company*.

■ There are additional government actions that come under the umbrella of privatisation including deregulation and the contracting out of services, like

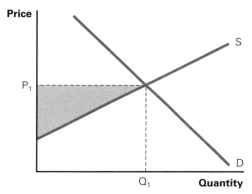

p

school meals and refuse collection, to private enterprise. Also, there are alternative ways of denationalising which have transferred assets to employees of the company or made a placing of the shares with an already existing private firm.

producer good: the name given to a good, like a component or a machine, which is made to be used by firms in the production of consumer goods and services.

producer surplus: the revenue received by the producer above that which would have brought the product onto the market for sale.

▓ In a market analysis, it is the difference between the *opportunity cost* of producing each unit and the market price of the product. This is represented in the diagram below by the shaded area above the supply curve and below the price line.

▓ *TIP* The market is in equilibrium where the producer surplus plus the *consumer surplus* is maximised.

product: a collective term for anything produced by a firm including goods, services, components and machines.

product differentiation: the attempt by a firm to create a brand image in the consumer's mind which separates its product from other similar products.

▓ This can be done by packaging, presentation and by *advertising* that stresses the actual or implied unique characteristics of the product. The more successful product differentiation is, the more inelastic the demand curve.

▓ *TIP* Watch adverts and note the different ways that firms try to differentiate their products.

production: the process of using the *factors of production* to create products for the consumer and producer.

production function: exists in various algebraic forms, the simplest of which is $Q = f(K,L)$ where Q is output and this is a function (f) of capital (K) and labour (L).

▓ Alternatively, it can be referred to as a ratio of inputs to output. Both formulations are related to a given time period.

production possibility curve/frontier/boundary: joins together the different combinations of consumer and capital products that can be produced if the economy is working at full capacity.

■ The economy cannot produce outside the boundary (Z), although economic growth can shift the boundary further out. If the economy is producing inside the boundary (Y), there are unemployed resources.

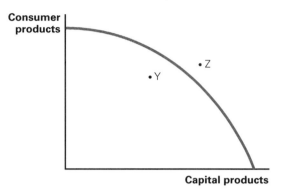

■ The shape of the curve represents the fact that there is a range of more and less efficient combinations of productive factors that can be used to produce both groups of products.

■ *TIP* Production possibility curves are commonly used in the explanation of *opportunity cost* and *economic growth*.

productive efficiency: exists when a firm is producing at *capacity output* or the lowest point on the average cost curve where MC = AC.

■ Along with *allocative efficiency* (P = MC) the two make up *economic efficiency*, which is illustrated in the long-run profit-maximising equilibrium of the firm in perfect competition.

profit: an economist's definition is the excess of revenue over costs where costs include the *normal profit* or cost of enterprise.

■ In contrast, the Inland Revenue does not allow for the cost of enterprise when identifying those profits that are taxable.

profit margin: the total profit as a percentage of total revenue or the excess of average revenue over average cost as a percentage of price.

profit-maximising rule: a firm's output equates *marginal cost* to *marginal revenue* when marginal cost is rising.

■ *TIP* Theories of the *firm* assume profit maximisation although, in a dynamic economy, the assumption can be questioned on two grounds. Do firms have the information to identify the profit-maximising position? And do all firms share this motivation, or are some motivated by other goals? See *sales maximisation hypothesis*.

progressive tax: when the marginal rate of tax is higher than the average rate of tax.

■ *Income tax* systems are usually progressive as politicians pursue policies to redistribute income. As people's incomes rise, so they pay a greater proportion of their income in tax.

propensity: a measure of the extent to which the change in an independent variable changes a dependent variable.

■ In economics, it is commonly used in the marginal and average form when the independent variable is income and the dependent variables include savings, taxation, imports and consumption.

property: anything owned by a person that has value.

■ *TIP* It includes tangible assets like cars, buildings and antiques, as well as intangible assets like patents and intellectual property — do not make the mistake of thinking that property only refers to buildings.

proportional tax: when the marginal and average rate of payment from a taxable source is the same.

■ In terms of *income tax*, a rate of 25% would produce a constant proportion of taxable income paid to the Inland Revenue.

protection: most commonly refers to the *tariffs, quotas* and other restrictions on international trade that protect domestic industry from foreign competition.

PSBR: see *public sector borrowing requirement.*

PSDR: see *public sector debt repayment.*

PSNCR: see *public sector borrowing requirement.*

public choice: an area of economic analysis concerned with applying economic principles to the political decision-making process in the non-market sector of the economy.

■ Among other things, it is used in the analysis of *public goods* and collective choice. Also, there is an interesting attempt to apply the rules of profit maximisation to the motive politicians have to maximise votes.

public enterprise: a description of government being directly involved in the allocation of resources to the provision of goods and services.

■ *e.g.* Nationalised industry.

public expenditure: combines the spending of local and national government and is divided into current expenditure which maintains the current level of service, and capital expenditure that increases the level of service.

■ *TIP* Do not confuse spending by the public, which is private expenditure, with expenditure by the government, which is public expenditure.

public finance: in its narrow sense, this defines the way in which the government raises money, mainly through taxation and borrowing, to pay for its expenditure programme.

■ In a wider sense, public finance can be concerned with analysing all the revenue and expenditure activities of government.

public good: a product for which there is a collective demand but, because it has the characteristics of being non-rival and non-excludable, it will not be produced in a free market economy.

▨ Non-rival means that if one person consumes the product, it does not reduce its availability to other people, while non-excludable means that if it is produced, then no one can be excluded from its use. It is generally agreed among economists that this is a good argument for taxing people to pay for the product.

▨ *e.g.* National defence, law and order, street lighting.

public joint stock company (also called 'public limited company' (plc)): a large private firm whose shares can be bought and sold by any member of the public through the stock exchange.

▨ *TIP* Do not confuse a public corporation (which is in the public sector of the economy) with a public joint stock company (which is in the private sector of the economy).

public limited company (plc): see *public joint stock company*.

public–private partnership: government and private firms joining together to resource a particular economic activity.

▨ This includes partial privatisations where only certain parts of an activity may have been attractive to the private sector. It was discussed in the case of the railways and the London Underground.

▨ *e.g.* The Millennium Dome.

public sector: all those economic activities that are owned or funded by central or local government.

▨ *e.g.* Public corporations including nationalised industries, the National Health Service and state education.

public sector borrowing requirement (PSBR) (also called the 'public sector net cash requirement' (PSNCR)): when the spending of the public sector (national and local government) is greater than the government income from taxation and other sources during any one year.

▨ The PSBR is financed by the sale of government securities and, year on year, this total is added to the *national debt.*

public sector debt repayment (PSDR): when the spending of the public sector (national and local government) is less than the government income from taxation and other sources during any one year, and the government chooses to repay the debt.

▨ A PSDR reduces the size of the *national debt.*

▨ *TIP* PSDRs are relatively rare as politicians usually agree that spending is preferable to debt repayment when it comes to attracting votes.

public sector net cash requirement (PSNCR): see *public sector borrowing requirement.*

purchasing power parity: when an amount of money in one country can be exchanged for a quantity of foreign currency, and the two amounts will buy identical baskets of products in both countries.

▨ This provided an early theory of exchange rate determination that was found to be wanting when measured against the actual exchange rate.

quantity theory of money: introduced by *Irving Fisher* in the publication *The Purchasing Power of Money* (1911), it stated that the identity $M.V = P.T$ is the equation of exchange where: M = stock of money; V = velocity of circulation of money; P = average price level; and T = number of transactions.

■ In its simplest form, V and T are constants while M is independent of the other three variables, meaning that a change in M has a direct effect on the average price level. The equation was developed by a number of economists and became a complex model, but in its simplest form and, with a few refinements, it is a useful learning tool. If M remains a stock, whereas $M.V$ is a flow over a given period of time equivalent to aggregate monetary demand, P is the average price level at the end of the time period, T is the number of transactions completed during the time period, and feedback loops occur over time, then:

■ *e.g. 1* Suppose, in a closed economy, a rise in M takes place at the *full employment* level of output, P will rise and this inflation may cause consumers to bring forward purchases. This increases the *velocity of circulation* of money, and P is forced to rise further.

■ *e.g.2* Suppose a fall in M causes a fall in P and T and this encourages consumers to put back purchases. This slows the velocity of circulation and reduces P and T further.

■ *TIP* Both examples can be used to offer one explanation as to why *inflation* and *deflation* rates seem to be higher than the original change in the stock of money.

quasi-economic rent: a temporary *economic rent*, or surplus over *transfer earning*, that will be eroded over time by market forces.

■ It occurs in labour markets when an increase in demand is associated with a supply of labour that is temporarily fixed.

■ *e.g.* When the NHS was set up, the demand for doctors and dentists rose rapidly as consumers increased their demand at zero price to where marginal utility was zero and total utility was maximised. The supply of these professionals involves up to 7 years' training and so there were high incomes available for several years. More recently, computer programmers, North Sea divers and Internet providers have seen a surge in demand and therefore an opportunity to earn quasi-economic rent.

q

quaternary industry: sometimes used to classify non-essential services.

▨ *e.g.* Entertainment and tourism.

quota: a term often applied to limits imposed on the quantity of imports of a particular type or from a particular country in order to protect domestic industry.

▨ As the quota imposes limits on supply to the market, it is usually associated with a rise in price which can benefit those firms with a share of the quota. Less common are export quotas which have been used in less developed countries to stabilise the earnings from certain commodity exports. Political pressure has been put on countries, particularly in the Far East, to impose a voluntary export restraint on products to the US and EU countries.

rate of interest: see *interest rate*.

rate of return: the earnings from capital invested in the form of physical capital or money capital.

■ The term also applies to the return on *human capital*, in which case it is possible to measure the cost of education as capital investment and the rate of return as a stream of future income earned over and above an income that could be earned by an uneducated person. The rate of return on units of physical capital employed is illustrated by the *marginal efficiency of capital*.

rational expectations theory: the assumption that individuals learn from experience and apply this learning to future events in the form of maximising behaviour.

■ This can be taken further to assume that people take a view about the costs of acquiring information up to the point where the *marginal cost* of this acquisition is equal to the expected future marginal benefits.

■ *e.g.* If people expect *inflation* to continue at a particular rate, this may cause them to bring forward their planned purchases as well as increase their wage target in negotiations.

rationing: a way of allocating resources which does not involve using the *price mechanism*.

■ Rationing in one form or another is likely to take place if the price is set below the equilibrium market price.

■ *e.g.* One of the failures of *command economies* was rationing by queuing. In the 1970s, citizens of Moscow were reported to be spending up to 4 hours a day queuing for products. War years usually involve widespread rationing of products, while events such as football cup finals involve limits on ticket allocations to clubs.

real: an important prefix to many economic terms that denotes output and removes the risk of *money illusion*, particularly where nominal measures change but real changes in output have not occurred or may even have occurred but in the opposite direction.

■ *e.g.* Measuring national income at constant prices produces real *national income*. Real wages tell a person what they can buy with their money. Real money balances measure the value of money holdings in terms of the products they can buy.

redistribution policy: an attempt by government to redistribute income and/or wealth by the use of taxation and expenditure policy.

▨ *Progressive taxation* targeted at the rich reduces their disposable income, while government expenditure, in the form of welfare payments, increases disposable income of the poor.

▨ *TIP* The controversial point about redistributive policies is the difference between the immediate effect and the longer-term outcome. In the case of income redistribution, welfare is likely to be raised because a pound taken from a rich person reduces total utility less than the gain of utility for the poorer person who receives it. However, the cost of administration and a longer-term effect on motivation and economic growth may both offset the immediate benefit. The *wealth effect* of a redistribution has an immediate benefit, but over the longer term the tax source is redistributed away and the total amount of income derived from wealth is relatively small, so its effect on living standards is likely to be relatively slight.

reflation: an expansion in *aggregate demand* that could be brought about by cutting *taxation*, raising *government expenditure*, increasing the *money supply* or cutting *interest rates*.

▨ Reflation may result in *inflation* or it may not if output expands at the same or a faster rate.

▨ *TIP* There is a debate between *monetarists* and Keynesians over the exact meaning of reflation which stems from their opposing views of the cause of inflation. Monetarists argue that a growth in money supply precedes inflation, so that any inflation is the result of reflation unmatched by a corresponding rise in output. However, Keynesians argue that at less than *full employment*, inflation is cost–push and that if the money supply does not rise to accommodate the *cost–push inflation*, then deflation has occurred.

regional policy: an approach by government to ironing out imbalances of income and employment in different parts of the country by attempting to stimulate depressed local economies.

▨ Government involvement in regional policies has met with considerable criticism over recent years, and there have been question marks over whether or not the overall effect has imposed more costs than benefits on society. Arguably, this has caused a downturn of activity in this area of government activity.

regressive taxation: when the proportion of a person's income paid in tax falls as their income rises.

▨ *e.g.* Any fixed rate expenditure tax such as *VAT*.

▨ *TIP* With regressive tax, people on higher incomes can still pay more tax in absolute terms, albeit less tax as a proportion of their rising income.

relative price: the *opportunity cost* of one product in terms of another product.

■ It is important to recognise that changes in relative price are the market signals which reallocate resources. These changes should not be confused with changes that could take place in *absolute prices,* say through inflation, which can have no effect on relative prices.

rent: strictly the reward to the owner of the *factor of production, land.*

■ Because all land resources were originally the free gift of nature, early economists looked upon rent as a surplus. The surplus existed because there were no costs of production involved. This idea of a surplus reward was then applied to all the productive factors that were paid more than their *transfer earning.* See *economic rent.*

resale price maintenance: when the producer of a good or service sets the price at which the retailer must sell the product.

■ The 1964 Resale Prices Act made resale price maintenance illegal, but postage stamps and newspapers are exceptions which are allowed to have their price determined by the supplier. It is, therefore, not worth looking for a discount at a Post Office or newsagent. Other products — particularly electrical goods and cars — are sold under a strict regime to try and maintain prices at retail outlets. Producers use various techniques, like establishing recommended retail prices or minimum advertised prices and, if these are ignored, retailers may find that the manufacturer refuses to supply them. Although against the law, these restrictions have been difficult to prove in the courts.

reserve base: the minimum level of *liquidity* held by banks and licensed deposit takers.

■ In the past, *banks* were given guidelines on a ratio of reserve assets to liabilities that they must hold. The easing of restrictions in the banking sector has allowed banks to make their own decisions on holding reserve assets, although there is still a requirement to maintain a non-operational cash deposit at the *Bank of England* equivalent to 0.5% of defined eligible liabilities. Banks and licensed deposit takers now establish their own reserve bases related to their customers' demand for liquidity.

retail price index (RPI): the most popular measure of changes in the value of *money* including, as it does, a change in the average price of a number of typical products in the average person's shopping basket.

■ The calculations are percentage changes in the prices of products added to or taken away from index numbers that were given a base number of 100. These numbers are then weighted to reflect the pattern of consumer expenditure. Over time, the typical shopping basket and the weights given to the items in it change so that new products are added and others are removed at regular intervals along with adjustments to weights for those items that remain in the basket. See also *underlying inflation.*

■ *TIP* When calculating an unweighted index, all the index numbers for each product are added together and then the total is divided by the number of products. Given a weighted index, the same process takes place except that the total is divided by the number of weights allocated not by the number of products involved.

revaluation: in a *fixed exchange rate* system a decision is made to increase the price of one currency to a higher fixed level relative to other currencies.

▨ *TIP* Although revaluation stresses a movement from one fixed rate to another, students should not fail to recognise that market forces still determine the exchange rate. It is intervention in the buying and selling of currency by the *central bank* that sustains the fixed rate. When the central bank's foreign currency reserves are growing excessively, then a currency revaluation is likely.

reverse dumping: when firms in one country sell their product at a higher price in a foreign market, usually to take advantage of a degree of *monopoly power*.

▨ Whereas *dumping* disadvantages domestic producers but is an advantage to consumers, the process in reverse advantages domestic producers but is a disadvantage to consumers.

▨ *e.g.* Foreign car prices in the UK.

reverse income tax: see *negative income tax*.

Ricardo, David (1772–1823): a classical economist credited with the early work on theories of *rent* and *comparative advantage*.

▨ Ricardo worked for many years in the City of London and earned enough to finance retirement at 42 so he could pursue his interests in economics and politics. He was particularly concerned with the process of analysis and the construction of models that had a practical use. He became an MP in 1819.

risk: the probability that something will be successful or profitable and the magnitude of the risk relative to possible outcomes.

▨ *e.g.* A large firm may risk £1 million of its £1 billion profit in a new venture which has a 1 in 10 probability of success. Set that against a small firm that risks bankruptcy by investing £10,000 in a new venture which has a 5 in 10 chance of success. Which firm is taking the greater risk?

risk averter: a person who makes economic decisions which involve little or no risk.

▨ *e.g.* People who are employees and have savings accounts.

risk taker: a person who makes economic decisions which involve a high risk.

▨ *e.g. Entrepreneurs* and speculators.

rival: a product characteristic when its consumption by one person reduces the quantity available for other people to consume.

▨ *Private goods* are rival in consumption. See *excludable*.

▨ *e.g.* Food and clothing.

road pricing: either a price to cover the full economic cost of road building and operation as if it was in the private sector of the economy, or a price paid by users to cover the external cost to others of road use.

▨ In the first case, pricing is aimed at achieving a more economically efficient allocation of resources, while in the second case, it is often considered as part of an integrated public sector transport policy aimed at reducing external costs such as road congestion. In both cases, pricing is used loosely to cover a variety of finance initiatives including purchase tax on vehicles, road fund licences, fuel taxes, road tolls and the possible use of electronic tagging systems.

Robbins, Lionel (1898–1984): Professor of Economics at the London School of Economics between 1929 and 1961 who is remembered for stressing the need to separate *normative economics* from *positive economics* as well as his often quoted definition of economics as 'the science which studies human behaviour as a relationship between ends and scarce means which have alternative uses'.

Rostow's growth model: introduced by Professor W. W. Rostow in 1961, it incorporated the following five stages of growth for a country:
- traditional society
- the preconditions to set up takeoff
- the takeoff
- the move to a mature economy
- mass consumption and production

RPI: see *retail price index.*

RPIX: see *underlying inflation.*

salary: the name given to a *wage* that is not dependent upon hours worked and is usually paid directly into a person's bank account each month.

sales maximisation hypothesis: an alternative theory to profit maximisation which is applied to large firms where there is a degree of separation between owners and managers such that the firm aims to maximise sales revenue given a profit constraint.

For reasons of status and salary, the managers of a company have incentive to make the company larger than the profit-maximising equilibrium. The profit target is an amount that is sufficient to satisfy shareholders who are usually disinterested in the way the company is run. Some firms have recognised this situation and — in trying to avoid it — force their managers to become share-holders in the company, to the extent that a significant proportion of their income is dependent upon the dividends paid to shareholders.

sales revenue maximisation: a more precise alternative theory to profit maximisation that involves output being expanded up to the point where *marginal revenue* is zero and total revenue is maximised.

sales tax: a collective term for those taxes raised on the price of a transaction in final demand.

e.g. Value added tax, customs duty, excise duty, stamp duty.

satisficing behaviour: an action in economics which is sufficient to satisfy the agent involved and does not result in maximising behaviour.

This is often used as an alternative theory to profit maximisation where the firm is satisfied by a certain level of profit and does not strive to achieve a higher attainable level.

e.g. The partners in a small firm may be satisfied to achieve a target reward and then substitute leisure for work.

savings: any income that is not spent on goods, services and investment products.

Savings may be withdrawn from the flow of income in the form of coins kept in a piggy bank, or they may be made available for investment through the purchase of savings products.

TIP In the financial sector, savings products are those which guarantee the return of the nominal value of the savings, while investment products put this

S

original sum at risk. This is why investment products carry a reminder that their value can go down as well as up.

scarcity: when there are insufficient products and productive factors to satisfy all consumer needs and therefore an allocative mechanism is required.

■ Without scarcity there would be no subject of economics as there would be no requirement to allocate resources.

■ *TIP* In economics, the term scarcity applies to all products except *free goods*. This means that all economic goods can be described by their relative scarcity. Therefore, a product which might be described as abundant by the layperson will be relatively less scarce to the economist.

Schumpeter, Joseph (1883–1950): born and educated in Austria, he spent most of his academic career in America and is remembered for his pioneering work on trade cycle analysis, *interest rates* and for his defence of *oligopoly* and *monopoly*.

■ On this last point, Schumpeter argued that oligopolies and monopolies are more conducive to innovation and growth than perfectly competitive firms. Therefore, over time, they bring about greater efficiency through lower costs and prices.

■ *TIP* If Schumpeter is right, then US and UK legislation regarding monopolies, mergers and restrictive practices needs redrafting.

SDRs: see *special drawing rights*.

search unemployment: see *frictional unemployment*.

seasonal adjustment: removing seasonal changes from statistics in order to identify the underlying trend.

■ *e.g.* Suppose that each July unemployment figures rose by 1% as the result of students registering as unemployed until they start employment or courses in October. If this seasonal factor is removed, then the underlying rise or fall can be identified.

seasonal unemployment: labour is laid off as the result of seasonal changes in people's demand for, and producers' ability to supply, certain types of product.

■ *e.g.* Construction workers can find themselves unemployed during the winter months, while the same happens to skiing instructors during the summer.

secondary industry: those firms which use the output of *primary industry* to manufacture goods.

■ *e.g.* Cars, clothes, computers.

securities: a wide range of relatively secure debt held as a financial asset by individuals and institutions.

■ *e.g.* Government short, medium and long-term debt, *bills of exchange*, local authority *bonds*, *share* certificates and *debentures*.

seepage: a flow of products from one market segment to another that reduces a firm's ability to price discriminate.

■ *e.g.* The ability of car manufacturers to maintain higher prices in the UK is being threatened by people ordering right-hand drive cars in Europe and driving them back to the UK.

services: the intangible products that satisfy consumer demand.

These products are the output of *tertiary industry* and are more important, by value, to the UK economy than the combined total of *primary industry* and *secondary industry*.

e.g. Banking, insurance, theatre, sporting events, holidays.

shadow price: an imputed value given to a product that does not have a market price and is most commonly used in *cost–benefit analysis*, particularly at the level of externalities.

share: proof of ownership that entitles the holder to dividends and shareholder rights relative to the number of shares held.

shareholder: the owner of shares.

share price: the current market price of a single unit of a firm's equity.

The price may vary from day to day and the asset value, *ceteris paribus*, move in the opposite direction to changes in interest rates.

shifts and movements: a shift in a supply or demand curve means that more or less of the product is supplied or demanded at the same price and should not be confused with a movement, where more or less is supplied or demanded as the result of a change in the price.

shoe leather costs of inflation: these occur when high *inflation* and high nominal rates of interest encourage people to hold a minimum active *money* balance, and therefore take more trips to the bank to change interest-bearing accounts into *cash*.

short run: the production time period over which a firm can make a partial reaction to changes in the market but is constrained by at least one *factor of production* that cannot be changed.

The action described above creates short-run marginal and average production and cost functions that are different from the *long run*.

sight deposit (also called 'demand deposit'): a chequeable account held at banks and other similar deposit-taking institutions that is distinct from other accounts in that funds can be used directly to make a purchase.

Sight deposits differ from instant access accounts that do not allow the holder to write a *cheque* but do offer the opportunity to draw cash or transfer funds immediately into a chequeable account.

Single European Act: introduced in 1987 with the aim of moulding the member countries of the *European Union* into a single indivisible market by the end of 1992.

The Act specifies economic cohesion by a free movement of all products and productive factors. In addition, political, welfare and legal arrangements were harmonised to produce social cohesion.

single European currency: the *euro* was introduced in January 1999 when those *European Union* countries which met the criteria for entry — and chose to join — fixed their currencies irreversibly to the European currency.

The perceived advantages of joining were the removal of exchange rate costs, the removal of the uncertainty which benefits speculators and imposes costs on traders, and the introduction of a European central bank that imposes price and interest rate stability throughout the EU. A year on, the UK had not joined despite meeting the criteria for membership. The disadvantages included the transition costs, the loss of exchange rate and interest rate flexibility and, therefore, the ability to deal with domestic economic shocks through domestic monetary policy.

Smith, Adam (1723–90): a philosopher and economist whose seminal book on markets and capitalism is the *Inquiry into the Nature and Causes of the Wealth of Nations* (1776).

■ Smith's account of the wealth of nations offers an explanation of how markets create an efficient allocation of resources through the 'invisible hand' that guides the actions of consumers and producers. Competition and the self-interested pursuit of profit leads to economic growth through the *division of labour*, technical progress and capital accumulation. Smith also recognised a role for government in the case of what are now recognised as *public goods* and the protection of *infant industry*.

snob effect (also called 'conspicuous consumption effect'): when certain products have the added characteristic of being able to display wealth only at high prices.

■ The result is that these products may attract customers at high prices and lose these same customers if the price is reduced so that the product can no longer be used to display wealth. It is, therefore, possible for this type of product to have a perversely sloping demand curve if a fall in price leads to a loss of customers due to the snob effect that is greater than the customers gained through a normal market response to a lower price.

■ *e.g.* Designer clothes.

social benefit: the total benefit from consuming a product which recognises the private benefit to the individual plus any external benefits to society.

■ *TIP* Do not confuse social benefit with external benefit. See *externality*.

Social Charter: an EU document designed to coordinate social legislation throughout the member countries.

■ The Charter covers a range of areas including health and safety; protection of children, elderly persons, adolescents and disabled persons; sexual equality; employment and remuneration; collective bargaining and the right to strike.

social cost: the total cost of producing a product which recognises the *private costs* to the firm plus any external costs to society.

■ *TIP* Do not confuse social cost with external cost. See *externality*.

social optimum: an allocation of resources that takes into account social costs and social benefits and occurs when a price is established for a product that equates the marginal social cost of production with the marginal social benefit from consumption.

social welfare: the wellbeing of society which includes a positive reference to *economic welfare* and *value judgements* regarding the way in which resources should be allocated to maximise social welfare.

soft loan: a loan where the interest rate is lower than the market rate or there is a period when no repayments are demanded.

■ Soft loans are usually made to a *developing country* as part of *foreign aid*.

sole proprietor (also called 'sole trader'): single person business where the owner and manager are one and the same.

■ The sole proprietor may also be the only employee in the *firm*, but can still use this descriptor if other people are employed in the business so long as there is only one owner.

special deposits: compulsory *cash* calls by the *Bank of England* to the *commercial banks* to place a percentage of their overall deposits in a frozen account at the *central bank*.

■ In the past, this was an important way of controlling the growth in monetary demand. Over recent years, use of this technique has remained dormant, although the Bank of England has retained the right to call for special deposits.

special drawing rights (SDRs): monetary assets created for member countries of the *International Monetary Fund* to boost their reserves of foreign currency.

specialisation of function: the separation of a job into the component parts which use different skills.

■ Labour can then be divided up and trained to a higher level of performance that increases output for the same factor inputs. This process was explained by *Adam Smith*. See also *division of labour*.

■ *TIP* Despite the advantages of this process, it has been recognised that the repetitive nature of some jobs can demotivate and alienate the workforce. Therefore, in order to enrich the working environment, many firms have taken advantage of developments in robotics to create machines that can do the simple jobs created by specialisation of function, leaving the more interesting and varied jobs to labour.

specific tax: a nominal tax placed upon each unit of output at the point of sale.

■ *e.g.* Excise duties such as 5p on a litre of petrol, 2p on a pint of beer, 30p on a bottle of wine.

■ *TIP* Remember that a rise in a specific tax shifts the market supply curve vertically upward and parallel to itself, whereas a percentage addition to the value of output causes the vertical separation between the two curves to increase as sales increase.

speculation: the process of buying or selling assets in the present only to reverse the process in the future and make a profit on a change in the value of the asset.

■ *TIP* Speculation requires the passage of time. Don't confuse it with *arbitrage* which notices different prices for assets at one point in time and makes a profit by simultaneous buying and selling decisions.

speculative demand for money: holding money in anticipation of a fall in price of a product or asset that has been targeted for purchase.

■ It is the only demand for money in Keynesian *liquidity preference theory* which is functionally related to a change in interest rates. This is because of the inverse relationship between asset values and interest rates. In Keynesian theory, *bond* prices represent asset values and when the rate of interest is low, the speculative demand for money is high as people anticipate a rise in rates and a fall in bond prices, which can then be bought at a lower price. When interest rates are high, the speculative demand for money is low as it is likely that a fall in rates raises bond prices and speculators therefore hold on to their bonds.

■ *TIP* If the Keynesian description is hard to understand, then think more generally about the process of holding back on a purchase in anticipation of a fall in price. Buying a bargain holiday at the last minute is a form of speculating with money.

spillover effect: another way of describing an *externality*, a *neighbourhood effect* or third-party effect from either production or consumption in the form of either an external cost or an external benefit.

spot market: that part of the *foreign exchange market* which deals in prices for immediate purchase and sale of currency.

■ *Commodity* markets — which quote forward prices — usually offer spot prices for immediate delivery as well.

stagflation: a situation where an economy is simultaneously suffering from inflation, low or negative growth and rising unemployment.

■ This occurred in the UK during the 1970s, and confounded Keynesian economists who had assumed a trade-off between more *inflation* and more employment or less inflation and more unemployment. Therefore, they were surprised to observe that attempts by government to boost aggregate demand caused unemployment to rise and inflation to accelerate.

stamp duty: a tax paid on the purchase of certain assets that gets its name from the stamp required on the document to show that the duty has been paid.

■ *e.g.* Purchase of shares and house purchase above an exempt limit.

standard of deferred payment: one of the four main functions of *money* which describes it as providing a basis for credit transactions so that when a deal is made, the exact extent of the future obligation is known.

■ *e.g.* Using a credit card requires this function as purchases today do not have to be settled for anything up to 2 months depending upon the day of the purchase relative to the settlement day.

standard of living: includes characteristics which are quantifiable, as in *goods* and *services* consumed, and also unquantifiable, such as low stress levels, pleasant climate, nice scenery etc.

■ The above characteristics can be separated into quantity and quality where measures of *gross national product* and *gross domestic product* can reflect the quantity aspect, while the *human development index* attempts to include factors that affect the quality of life.

■ *TIP* A popular examination question looks at the extent to which national income statistics can reflect differences in living standards between countries and changes in living standards over time in the same country.

steady state growth: a description in growth theory which assumes that all real variables change at a constant rate which can be positive, negative or zero.

▨ *e.g.* Steady state growth would exist in an economy where capital is growing at 5% each year, while the labour force is growing at 2% each year.

▨ *TIP* This is different from a balanced growth where capital and labour grow by the same percentage each year.

sterling: the name given to the UK currency to distinguish it, particularly in *foreign exchange markets*, from other countries which use a pound for their currency unit.

stock: materials, work in progress and finished products held by a firm to guard against unexpected changes and to respond to expected changes in product demand.

▨ At the aggregate level, and recorded in *national income* statistics, the value of stock is an important indication of changes in economic activity.

stock appreciation: a nominal increase in the value of stock as the result of a rise in price of the product often, but not always, caused by *inflation*.

stock exchange: the market that deals in second-hand securities, therefore providing a degree of liquidity for assets like company shares and undated government debt which have no maturity date.

▨ *e.g.* London stock exchange, New York stock exchange.

▨ *TIP* Do not make the mistake of referring to this market as the one that raises finance for industry. It only deals in second-hand securities, although its presence makes a successful issue of shares through the primary market more likely.

store of value: one of the four main functions of *money* that requires it to act as a repository for conserving the value of purchasing power.

▨ *Inflation* damages the ability of money to carry out this function. Modern forms of money have no inherent value and an accelerating rate of inflation encourages people to exchange money for real assets and ultimately to conduct trade in items, like gold, that have a value in use as well as a value in exchange.

structural unemployment: labour laid off when there is a decline in an important industry in a particular region and, although job vacancies exist elsewhere, there is a mismatch of supply and demand for labour through its occupational and geographical immobility.

▨ *e.g.* Coal mining in Wales and shipbuilding on Tyneside.

subnormal profit: a surplus income to the entrepreneur but below the normal profit that is the minimum required to keep the firm in the industry in the long run.

subsidy: a payment, usually made by government, to a firm that has the effect of reducing its costs of production.

▨ This may be done to keep down prices of essential products, to lower prices of *merit goods* that have external benefits, to support farm incomes or to maintain employment in a loss-making firm.

S

■ *TIP* Remember, a subsidy shifts *supply curves* to the right while an *indirect tax* shifts them to the left.

subsistence: a situation where a person's access to resources provides the minimum required to sustain life.

■ Subsistence societies are usually agriculturally based and produce enough food to survive but no surplus to trade for less essential products.

substitute: a product or productive factor that can replace another product or productive factor in the process of production or consumption.

■ Substitutes have a positive cross elasticity of demand such that a rise in the price of one increases demand for the other.

■ *e.g.* The consumer could choose gas or electricity, Ford or Vauxhall cars, while the producer may choose to use labour or machines to provide the same product.

substitution effect of a price change: when there is a rise or fall in the price of a product, the consumer receives a decrease or an increase in the *utility* derived from each unit of money spent on the product and therefore rearranges demand to maximise utility.

■ This is distinct from the *income effect of a price change*. For all products, the substitution effect is always negative such that a fall in price leads to an increase in demand as consumers realise an increase in the satisfaction they derive from each unit of money spent on the product.

■ *TIP* Remember that price changes have simultaneous effects on substitution and real income, and because the substitution effect is the same for all products, it is the income effect which determines whether a product is *normal*, *inferior* or *Giffen*.

sunk cost: non-recoverable costs when a firm leaves an industry.

■ The knowledge that there are significant sunk costs in an industry acts as a barrier both to entry and to exit.

■ *e.g.* Many start-up costs such as marketing and research and development.

superior product: a normal product that, by definition, has an inferior alternative.

■ Both superior and *inferior products* can only exist relative to each other and may involve a degree of subjective judgement on the part of each individual consumer.

■ *e.g.* In my opinion, beer is superior to lager and Charlton Athletic is superior to Manchester United.

supernormal profit: see *excessive profit*.

supply: the quantity produced over a given period of time at a given price by a firm, a group of firms which produce a similar product for a market, or all the firms which produce a country's total output or *aggregate supply*.

supply curve: the functional relationship between a change in price and a change in the quantity supplied by producers.

■ It is conventional to illustrate this function with price on the vertical axis and quantity on the horizontal axis. The normal shape for a supply curve is upward-sloping from left to right, as illustrated below.

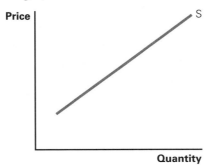

supply curve for labour: the functional relationship between changes in a particular wage rate and the supply of labour to a particular labour market.

■ The normal relationship is that a rise in wages in one labour market, *ceteris paribus*, increases the supply of labour to that market, as illustrated below.

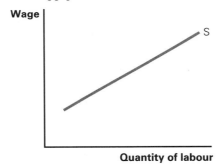

supply of effort curve: see *backward bending supply curve of labour.*

supply side economics: the solutions to problems of high *unemployment* or low, zero or negative *economic growth* are to be found on the supply side of the economy and not, as the Keynesian economists suggest, on the demand side.

■ Attention is focused on the factors which inhibit the efficient allocation of resources to the production and exchange of goods and services, and the application of policies to eliminate these constraints. Therefore, supply side policies would not involve any deliberate change to the overall level of *aggregate demand.*

■ *e.g.* Supply side policies could include deregulation, promotion of competition, privatisation, reinforcement of private property rights, changes to marginal tax rates, profit-related pay, reduction in national insurance payments, improved employee training etc.

■ *TIP* There is a significant enough debate between supply side and demand side economists for it to be a popular examination topic.

S

sustainability: a criterion for judging whether current economic actions can produce benefits which can be replicated into the future.

In terms of environmental actions, it means using renewable resources at a rate equal to or below their ability to regenerate. In terms of government actions, it means that capital expenditure generates sustainable current expenditure that at least produces *social benefits* to cover *social costs*. Economic growth in less developed countries is being looked at from the viewpoint of sustainable development, so that growth industries, like tourism, do not upset the delicate balances in the ecosystem.

tangible product: a *good* with a physical presence as opposed to a *service* which is described as an intangible product.

tariff: a tax placed upon an import into the country.

▨ A tariff may be a specific tax or an *ad valorem tax* imposed for a variety of reasons. The most common economic arguments used are protection against *dumping* and promotion of an *infant industry*.

taxable income: that part of an income which is legally liable to pay tax.

▨ In the case of *income tax* or *corporation tax* it is total income minus allowances and expenses.

▨ *e.g.* An individual's total income can have allowances — for being married, having a mortgage, paying into a pension, incurring business expenses — deducted before tax has to be paid.

taxation: the range of taxes that individuals and organisations are legally liable to pay in order to finance government expenditure.

tax avoidance: a legal way of using the system of allowances and expenses to reduce taxable income at the level of the individual and the firm.

▨ *TIP* Do not confuse this with *tax evasion*, which is an illegal activity.

tax burden: a reference to the proportion of income paid in tax where the income could be an individual income or the national income.

▨ Governments often claim to be reducing taxation when, in fact, they have reduced *income tax* but increased other taxes so that the overall tax burden has increased.

tax evasion: not paying the tax that is legally due and — whether the evasion is by design or through ignorance — a person or organisation remains liable to prosecution.

▨ *e.g.* An individual may not declare all his or her income to the Inland Revenue or may try to claim allowances and expenses to which he or she is not entitled.

▨ *TIP* Do not confuse this with *tax avoidance* which is a legal activity.

tax haven (also called 'tax shelter'): places or countries with lower tax rates, where rich individuals or international firms may try to protect their income or wealth from domestic taxation.

▨ *e.g.* Cayman Islands.

tax incidence: where the burden of taxation finally settles. See *incidence of taxation*.

tax revenue: a reference to the money paid to government from the various types of tax.

tax shelter: see *tax haven*.

tax threshold: the point at which income becomes liable to taxation.

■ *TIP* It is interesting to ask anyone whose income is not sufficient to reach the income tax threshold, if they pay tax. The answer is often 'no', as they forget the *expenditure taxes* paid when spending an income.

technical efficiency: an alternative way of describing *productive efficiency* where firms are producing at the lowest point on their average cost curves.

technical progress: this takes place when technical change goes through the process of *innovation* such that new products may be produced or more efficient ways of producing old products may be implemented.

technical unemployment: labour laid off as the result of *technical progress* when new machines replace people in the productive process, or new skills are required to implement the new developments.

terms of trade: a measure of how export prices have changed relative to import prices, while the real terms of trade show the quantity of *exports* that can be exchanged for a given quantity of *imports*.

■ The formula is:

$$\text{terms of trade} = \frac{\text{index number showing the average price of exports}}{\text{index number showing the average price of imports}} \times 100$$

■ *e.g.* In the base year (year 1) the terms of trade are 100. Suppose in year 2 export prices rise by 10% and import prices by 25%, the terms of trade are:

$$\frac{110}{125} \times 100 = 88$$

This fall is described as unfavourable because more exports have to be sold to buy the same quantity of imports. Then, in year 3, the export index rises to 125 while the import index rises to 130:

$$\frac{125}{130} \times 100 = 96.2$$

The rise from 88 to 96.2 is a favourable movement because fewer exports have to be sold to buy the same quantity of imports.

■ *TIP* There are several common misunderstandings regarding the terms of trade. First, the description favourable or unfavourable relates to whether the figure is rising or falling, as in the example above. It is not related to whether the number is above or below 100. Second, the terms of trade are only a price or quantity ratio. They say nothing about the value of export or import sales, so changes in the terms of trade reveal nothing about what is happening on the *balance of payments*. This means that a favourable movement in the terms of trade may or may not have a favourable effect on the balance of payments. The effect of a change in the terms of trade on the balance of payments will depend upon the price elasticities of demand for imports and exports.

tertiary industry: those firms which use the product of *primary industry* and *secondary industry* to produce services.

■ *e.g.* Banking, insurance, tourism.

tight policy: the government using its *fiscal policy* or *monetary policy* to restrict *aggregate demand*, usually to keep *inflation* under control and stop the economy from overheating.

■ If the description refers to monetary policy, then money supply may be slowed down or reduced and/or interest rates raised. If fiscal policy is referred to, then a rise in tax and/or a fall in government expenditure may be used.

■ *TIP* The tight policy description may vary depending upon whether Keynesians or monetarists are using the term.

till money: the cash kept at *commercial banks* to satisfy everyday customer demand for *liquidity.*

■ If there are no other constraints on bank lending, then the demand for till money acts as a constraint on the amount of loans a bank can create.

time-lag: the delay between a change in an independent variable and its effect upon the dependent variable.

■ *e.g.* Monetarists argue that an increase in the money supply may take up to 2 years before it affects inflation.

■ *TIP* In simple economic models, reactions are assumed to be instantaneous. However, the introduction of the time-lag produces a level of complexity that moves one step closer to reality.

time series data: statistical information on an economic variable collected at pre-defined intervals over a period of time.

■ The most common intervals are months, quarters and years.

■ *e.g.* Yearly national income statistics, quarterly production figures, monthly inflation data.

token money: all forms of *money* that have *value in exchange* but no *value in use*.

■ In the past, money in the form of gold *coins* was not token money because it had inherent value, i.e. could be used to make jewellery.

■ *e.g.* Modern forms of token money include *notes*, *cheques* and *credit cards*.

toll: a payment made to use certain roads and bridges.

■ These are less common in the UK than in Europe where many motorways charge the user a toll.

■ *e.g.* A toll is paid to cross the River Thames at Dartford, using the bridge or tunnel.

■ *TIP* Tolls are often discussed as a form of road pricing that makes drivers more responsive to market forces and helps deal with the external costs of road use.

total currency flow: on the *balance of payments* it is equal and opposite to the total official financing of the account, such that a positive flow is likely to increase *foreign exchange reserves* and a negative flow is likely to reduce these reserves.

track costs: in transport economics, the cost of constructing and running a transport network shared out among the users of that route.

■ The issue is to compare the track costs per user with their contribution to those costs through taxes and direct payments. This helps determine a level of efficiency in resource allocation to the various *transport modes*.

trade: where people exchange products, either directly through *barter* or indirectly through the medium of *money*, in the hope of achieving mutual advantage.

■ The process of trade allows the *specialisation of function*, the *division of labour* and *economies of scale* to increase output per unit of input and expand the variety of consumer products.

trade barrier: a restriction on the free movement of products, usually between countries, by using *tariffs*, *quotas* and legal prohibition.

■ Although economic reasons such as the prevention of *dumping* and the protection of *infant industry* are put forward, there are many non-economic reasons for barriers that impede trade and the aim of GATT/WTO is to reduce these barriers to *free trade*. See *General Agreement on Tariffs and Trade*.

trade creation: new trade created by a change in the trade barriers between countries.

■ Usually, this process is *trade liberalisation* and the target is a reallocation of resources to create more trade than it diverts.

■ *e.g.* When the UK joined the European Economic Community in 1973, new trade was created in Europe and diverted from other countries, particularly those in the Commonwealth.

trade diversion: trade lost during a change in the trade barriers between countries.

■ Even if the process of *trade liberalisation* leads to net trade creation, it is likely that some trade diversion will have taken place as relative product prices are changed and/or new trade routes are opened up by adjustments to trade barriers.

trade gap: a common reference to the difference, on the *balance of trade*, between the value of exported and imported goods only.

■ The UK trade gap is inevitably a deficit, and therefore trade gap and deficit have mistakenly been understood to mean the same thing. However, a trade gap could also be a reference to a surplus.

■ *TIP* A lot of criticism of the UK economic performance is related to the persistent trade gap. However, it should be recognised that by far the more important gap is on the current balance which is the difference between exported and imported goods and services.

trade liberalisation: the process of reducing trade barriers throughout the world to take full advantage of the perceived benefits of free trade.

■ Over recent years, the less developed countries have been particularly keen to push, through the *World Trade Organisation*, for more open markets in the more developed world, with particular reference to the EU's *Common Agriculture Policy*.

trade-off: an action that results from the fundamental *economic problem* of *scarcity* and is recognised in the *opportunity cost* that manifests itself when choices are exercised.

In *macroeconomics*, government actions are often described as trade-offs between more of one thing and less of another.

e.g. More *economic growth*, less stability on the *balance of payments*; more *unemployment*, less *inflation*; more equality, less efficiency.

trade union: an organisation of workers financed by membership fees and responsible for organising the workforce, developing procedures for dealing with grievances, providing information regarding pay and job opportunities, monitoring the industrial relations policy of corporate management and bargaining collectively for wages and job protection.

There are various types of union including: a company union that represents every grade of labour within one firm; a craft union that represents a group of similarly skilled workers; an industrial union which covers all employees in a single industry; and a general union that represents a spread of similar employees across a range of occupations and/or industries.

transactions demand for money: holding *money* for the purpose of buying *goods, services* or *assets*.

The amount of money held is dependent upon the income of the person and the frequency of intervals between payments. A person who receives a monthly salary normally holds a higher average money balance for transactions than a person who receives a weekly wage. In Keynesian *liquidity preference theory*, this motive and the *precautionary demand for money* are active balances which are related to changes in *national income*, while the *speculative demand for money* is an idle balance that is related to changes in the rate of interest.

transfer earnings: the minimum earnings required by a *factor of production* to keep that factor in its current use.

e.g. If a next best occupation paid £25,000 a year and the person currently earned £35,000 a year, then the transfer earning is £25,000 and the surplus £10,000 is referred to as *economic rent*. Also the *normal profit* of an *entrepreneur* is a transfer earning.

TIP Do not confuse transfer earnings with *transfer payments*.

transfer payment: usually paid to an individual by government, it does not require any productive effort.

e.g. Welfare payments, state pensions and student grants.

TIP Do not confuse transfer payments with *transfer earnings*.

transitional economy: a country that is in the process of changing from a centrally controlled to a more market-orientated capitalist structure.

e.g. The countries of the former Soviet Union, other East European countries and China.

TIP Of the examples listed above, China is moving towards economic freedom without any corresponding move to liberate its political structure, whereas the other countries are pushing political and economic freedoms in tandem. When analysing transitional economies, an additional dimension for investigation is the cost of transition.

transmission mechanism: the process of how a change in one independent economic variable works through to a change in a dependent variable.

▦ It is often used to describe how a change in money stock works through the economy to change nominal and/or real national income.

transparency: this exists when there is perfect information available to all the parties in a product or asset transaction.

▦ Lack of transparency exists when deals take place without all the relevant information. *Advertising* is often designed to create deals that are less than transparent when certain product characteristics are highlighted while others are hidden.

▦ *TIP* Politicians have often admitted, after the event, to being less than entirely truthful so as not to have an adverse effect on the exchange rate.

transport economics: a study of the allocation of resources to the various *transport modes*.

▦ This is made difficult by the problem of whether or not the provision of transport networks is a *public good* or a *private good*. Consideration of the degree to which the characteristics of rivalry and excludability are present and a valuation of external costs such as pollution and congestion are necessary.

transport modes: a reference to whether people or products are moved from place to place using roads, railways, waterways, sea lanes, airways, pipelines or communication channels.

Treasury: arguably the most important department of the UK government in that it manages economic policy.

▦ The Treasury is responsible for producing the annual budget statement after listening to representations from government ministers during the annual 'spending round'. It is the direct responsibility of the *Chancellor of the Exchequer* and is ultimately the responsibility of the Prime Minister who is First Lord of the Treasury.

Treasury bill: government debt, issued at a discount to its face value in 90 days time, which is usually bought and sold on the *discount market* and is a short-term instrument that helps government manage the mismatch of its revenues and expenditure throughout the year.

▦ Treasury bills are an important source of *liquidity* for the *commercial banks* and therefore play an important role in government's economic management through its monetary policy.

Treaty of Rome: the original agreement that set up the European Economic Community, now known as the *European Union*.

▦ The original six members in 1958 were Belgium, France, Germany, Italy, Luxembourg and the Netherlands, with the UK, Denmark and Ireland joining in 1973.

unanticipated inflation: the actual rate of *inflation* minus the anticipated or expected rate of inflation.

■ This is important because the current action of producers and consumers depends, to a degree, on their anticipation of future inflation rates. Some economists argue that unanticipated higher rates of inflation may have caused a temporary rise in *output* which is reversed when the higher inflation occurs. *Anticipated inflation* can affect current spending by consumers, wage negotiations and investment decisions, all of which will be distorted by unanticipated inflation.

under-full employment equilibrium: a Keynesian interpretation of a situation where the economy settles at a high level of *unemployment* which is relatively stable but politically unacceptable.

■ The solution is to raise the level of *aggregate demand* through a *budget deficit* which increases government expenditure and/or reduces taxation to a point where the *full employment* equilibrium is achieved.

■ *TIP* The alternative point of view is that any level of unemployment which is politically unacceptable must be tackled by *supply side* policies that shift the natural rate of unemployment to a lower level.

underlying inflation: in the UK, it is a measure of price rises using the RPIX, which is the *retail price index* minus the change in mortgage interest rates.

undervalued currency: when a *fixed exchange rate* is lower than the rate that would exist in a *free market* and therefore foreign exchange reserves continue to grow.

■ In a fixed exchange rate system, a persistent current account surplus is usually an illustration of an undervalued currency. In a *floating exchange rate* system, an undervalued currency is less likely to persist, although it is possible for a country to maintain an undervalued level by using a low interest rate policy and foreign investment to produce an offsetting deficit on the capital account.

underwriter: someone who takes on a business risk for a fee.

■ *e.g.* For an issue of new shares, *merchant banks* usually underwrite all or part of the issue by agreeing to buy all or some of the unsold shares at the flotation price.

unemployment: a reference to any unused *factors of production*, although it is more commonly a reference to *labour* that is willing and able to work but is not in employment.

■ Unemployed labour can be further categorised into: casual — where work is irregular; *cyclical* — related to phases of the trade cycle; *disguised* — wives or husbands who become unemployed but do not register as such and rely on their partners' incomes; *demand deficient* — Keynesian *under-full employment equilibrium*; export — fall in demand from foreign markets; *frictional* — due to labour immobility; *seasonal* — where work depends on the time of the year; *search* — when labour is between jobs; *structural* — when an important industry declines, usually in a specific region; *technical* — new processes; unemployable — mentally or physically unable to work; voluntary — living off welfare benefits or inherited wealth.

■ *TIP* The different categories identify the fact that at full employment there will always be some unemployment and that there can be no one answer to the problem of unemployment.

unemployment benefit (also called 'jobseekers' allowance'): in the UK it is paid for a maximum of 6 months to those people who are unemployed, after which they have to apply for other welfare benefits.

unemployment rate: officially calculated as the percentage of the labour force which is registered as unemployed.

■ As economists have pointed out, this number can be significantly different from the actual number of people who are not, but would like to be, actively employed in the production of *goods* and *services*.

unit cost: the cost of producing a single item. See *average cost*.

unit labour cost: indicates comparative efficiency by measuring the proportion of *labour* costs to all other costs involved in producing a unit of output.

unit of account: one of the four main functions of *money* which recognises its ability to measure, record and compare the value of products.

urban economics: applies the tools of economic analysis to cities and towns, looking particularly at location and problems of urban transport, urban blight, urban regeneration and urban public services.

util: a measure of *utility* or consumer satisfaction and, although it has little practical significance except as an illustration of rank order, it is useful in conveying a theoretical meaning to some consumer theory, particularly when it is used as a measure for *marginal utility*.

utility: a reference to the usefulness or satisfaction which is derived from the consumption of a *good* or *service*, and the fact that someone is prepared to acquire and consume a product is sufficient and necessary proof of it having utility.

utility maximisation: an assumption in consumer theory which means that a rational consumer exercises choice in a pattern of expenditure that will maximise total satisfaction.

utility regulator: government-sponsored groups with the power to enforce regulatory action on the former publicly-owned utilities.

■ The *privatised* utilities that provide basic products — such as energy, telecommunications, transport and water — have a tendency towards natural monopolies and the utility regulators are there to ensure these new entrants to private enterprise do not abuse their status.

■ *e.g.* Electricity, OFFER; water, OFWAT; gas, OFGAS; telecommunications, OFTEL; railways, ORR and OPRAF.

value/value in exchange/value in use: an item's value can be looked at in terms of either/or both its exchange value, where it is recognised in monetary units, or units of another product and/or its inherent value, which can be identified in its value in use to one or more consumers.

■ Some products can have a value in use to one consumer but have no value in exchange, as in the case of something that is described as having only sentimental value to one person. In this situation, the value is synonymous with the *utility* that one person derives from the product. In contrast, modern *money* has value in exchange but no inherent value as it cannot be used for anything other than to be passed on sooner or later in exchange. However, most products have both elements of value, including early forms of money — like gold — which had exchange value as well as being inherently valuable in that jewellery could be made from it.

value added: the monetary contribution made to the value of a product as it passes through the various stages of production.

■ *e.g.* Firm A mined and sold £1,000 of raw materials to Firm B which made components that it sold to Firm C for £3,000. If Firm C assembled the final product and sold it to the consumer for £7,000, then:

Firm A added value = £1,000

Firm B added value = £2,000

Firm C added value = £4,000

value added tax (VAT): a percentage tax added to the price of a product and paid to Customs and Excise by the producer.

■ The tax is paid at each stage in the production process as value is added to the product, and it can be claimed back at the next stage in the process until it is finally paid to Customs and Excise by the consumer of the product.

■ *e.g.* Using the example under 'value added' and assuming VAT at 17.5%:

Firm A sells its output to Firm B for £1,117.50p and pays £117.50p VAT.

Firm B claims back £117.50p VAT when it sells its output to Firm C for £3,525, paying £525 VAT.

Firm C claims back £525 VAT when it sells its output to the consumer for £8,225, paying £1,225 VAT.

▓ After claim backs, each firm pays Customs and Excise:

$$
\begin{array}{lll}
\text{Firm A} & = & £117.50 \\
\text{Firm B} & = & £407.50 \\
\text{Firm C} & = & \underline{£700.00} \\
\text{Total VAT} & = & £1,225.00
\end{array}
$$

value judgement: an opinion based upon a belief rather than factual evidence and usually referred to as a *normative* statement.

▓ This means that it is possible to have an opinion which is not a value judgement if it is based on factual evidence. In this case, it is a positive statement. If economic decisions are based upon perfect knowledge, then there is no room for value judgements. However, the more imperfect knowledge is, the greater the need to involve value judgements in decision-making.

variable cost of production: a cost that is zero if nothing is produced and then varies with changes in output.

▓ In the short run, some costs are fixed while others are variable, whereas in the *long run* all costs are variable.

variable factors of production: factors that can be varied in the production process over the *short run*, when at least one *factor of production* is fixed.

▓ Over the *long run*, all factors of production are variable.

variable proportions (law of): see *diminishing marginal returns.*

VAT: see *value added tax.*

Veblen effect: named after the American economist Thorstein Veblen (1857–1929), it explains why demand curves for certain products may be perverse (upward-sloping from left to right).

▓ There are two slightly different interpretations of the Veblen effect. First, the *snob effect* or conspicuous consumption situation, where higher prices can be used to display wealth and attract more buyers — a situation which is reversed when prices fall. Second, a case where consumers interpret a fall in price as a reduction in the quality of a product and therefore reduce demand, while an increase in price is interpreted as a rise in quality which attracts more demand.

velocity of circulation: the average number of times one unit of *money* is used over a given time period.

▓ The *quantity theory of money*, $M.V = P.T$, can be rearranged to determine velocity of circulation as $V = P.T/M$.

▓ The average price level (P) multiplied by the number of transactions (T) divided by the stock of money (M) equals the velocity of circulation of money. See *quantity theory of money.*

vertical integration: when a firm expands through the stages of production, usually by taking over another firm.

▓ If the expansion is towards the retail end of the market, then it is described as forward integration, whereas if it is towards the raw material supplier, then it is described as backward integration. The motivation for doing this can vary including lower unit costs, higher profits, greater price security or diversity, or more stability in terms of control over raw material supplies or retail outlets.

▨ *e.g.* Forward integration is a manufacturer of pine furniture opening a retail store. Backward integration is a chain of public houses buying into a brewery.

▨ *TIP* Remember that horizontal integration is expansion at the same stage of the production process, while vertical integration is expansion across the stages.

vertical mobility: see *occupational mobility.*

very long run refers to the time it takes for supply conditions to change as a result of *technical progress.*

▨ It is the only time period when unit costs of production can fall while output is constant. In other words, the average cost of production curve shifts vertically downward. In the other production time periods, technical progress is held constant.

very short run: sometimes referred to as the momentary period, this is when all factors of production are fixed and therefore cannot make any response to a change in the condition of demand.

▨ *e.g.* A firm may have an agreement with its workforce that there has to be at least 24 hours notice of any change in working practices.

▨ *TIP* Remember that all the production time periods are only loosely related to calendar time and vary considerably from one firm to another and from one industry to another.

visible balance: see *balance of trade.*

voucher scheme: more often talked about than used, this is a redistributive technique where the government provides poorer people with vouchers that can only be exchanged for a specific product.

▨ *e.g.* The UK has used education vouchers, while the US has used food stamps for the poor.

wage: the financial reward to the productive factor *labour.*

▨ If a wage is paid over periods longer than a week and is independent of hours worked, it is usually referred to as a *salary*. The nominal wage is measured in units of *money* while the real wage is a measure in terms of the goods and services that can be purchased. Changes in nominal wages often create *money illusion* because people often respond as if *real* wages have changed. In reality, nominal and real wages can move in opposite directions.

wage differential: the difference in the average level of wage between groups of employees in the same firm, in different firms, in different parts of the country, in different labour markets, or in different age, gender or racial categories.

▨ *TIP* Understanding and explaining these differences is a popular source of examination questions.

wage drift: where a gap appears between officially agreed wage rates and the actual earnings of workers.

▨ This can result from a situation where local *labour market* conditions vary considerably from the average conditions across the country.

wage–price spiral: wage rises push up prices which, in turn, encourage labour to ask for even higher wages which push up prices even higher and so on.

wage rate: the financial reward to the productive factor *labour* measured over a specific period of time.

Wall Street Crash: the fall in *share* prices on the New York stock exchange in 1929 after sustained rises during the 1920s.

▨ There are two different interpretations of the place of the Wall Street Crash in economic history. *Galbraith*, among others, suggested it was the cause of the *Great Depression* which lasted until the Second World War. In contrast, *Friedman* suggested that it was no more than a major correction in share prices that had become overvalued, while the cause of the depression was the failure of the *Federal Reserve* to maintain *liquidity* in a banking system that had made loans to speculators which became unsecured when share prices fell.

wealth: the value of a stock of *assets* at any one point in time.

▨ To an individual, wealth is everything he or she owns that has value. This can include *capital*, financial assets and products which have a *value in exchange*.

Personal belongings that have nothing other than sentimental value to the owner would be excluded from a measure of wealth. The distribution of wealth is very uneven, mainly due to the distortion caused by inherited wealth. However, the distribution of income is significantly more evenly distributed than it was in the past.

wealth effect: people feel better off as a result of an increase in the value of their *assets* and are therefore likely to increase their demand for *products*.

▓ Initially, the idea was introduced by Gottfried Haberler in 1941 and referred to a situation where money increased in value during a *recession* such that people with excess real *money* balances would choose to spend, thus boosting *aggregate demand*. This wealth effect became known as the real balance effect. More recently, a wealth-induced increase in spending has been related to the sustained growth of asset values. This current interpretation of the wealth effect has its downside when *asset* values fall and people are likely to reduce their expenditure on current products.

wealth tax: a payment to government based upon a valuation of what a person owns.

▓ Various wealth taxes were discussed over the years, and the UK has come close to making a decision that would shift the balance of taxation away from income towards wealth. However, the change has never been introduced due to a number of criticisms. First, it was difficult to distinguish the source of wealth i.e. *capital gains*, inheritance, gambling, high income and saving. Second, it could have disincentive effects on capital accumulation and adversely affect *economic growth*. Third, the more successful the tax is at redistributing wealth, the more it destroys the tax source.

wear and tear (also called 'deterioration'): refers to that part of capital depreciation which takes place through use as opposed to the loss in value that results from *obsolescence*.

weighted average: allocating weights which reflect the importance of each number in a series of numbers before the average is calculated.

▓ In economic analysis, it is used to produce a more realistic answer when the numbers, from which the average is to be calculated, are not of equal importance.

Products	Index number	Weights	Weighted index number
A	120	2	240
B	80	3	240
C	160	5	800
	3/360		10/1,280
	= 120 unweighted average		= 128 weighted average

▓ *e.g.* Assume a *retail price index* includes only three products. Product A receives 20% of consumer expenditure and has an *index number* of 120, product B receives 30% of consumer expenditure and has an index number of 80 and product C receives 50% of consumer expenditure and has an index number of 160. The table on p. 152 shows the difference between an unweighted average and a weighted average where the weights are allocated in proportion to the pattern of consumption.

▓ The weighted average is higher than the unweighted average because the heaviest weight is on the number that has changed the most.

▓ *TIP* The unweighted average divides the total by the number of products (3), while the unweighted average divides the total by the number of weights allocated (10).

welfare economics: a branch of economics that looks at the positive and *normative* aspects of people's wellbeing and how their situation can be improved. See *economic welfare* and *social welfare*.

welfare state: in its narrowest sense, this refers to the education, health and social security provision that was set up in the UK after the Second World War to help, particularly, those people in need.

▓ The welfare state targets the poor, the elderly, children in need, the sick and the unemployed. Over recent years, it has been threatened by attempts to streamline services, cut costs and avoid raising the taxes required to cope with an ageing population. In a more general sense, it can be argued that all the activities of government are part of a welfare state in as much as they aim to promote social and economic welfare.

windfall gain: an unexpected gain in the income or wealth of an individual or organisation.

▓ *e.g.* An individual receiving free shares when a building society demutualises; a firm receiving a one-off boost to profits as the result of an unexpected event.

withdrawal: see *leakage*.

work: the process whereby *factors of production* forego leisure time (down time) to produce goods and services.

working capital: current assets minus current liabilities.

▓ It gives an indication of a firm's *liquidity* and long-term viability.

work in progress: the value of products which are incomplete at any particular point in time when accounts are drawn up.

▓ It comprises one element of a firm's stock that also includes raw materials and unsold finished products.

World Bank: see *International Bank for Reconstruction and Development*.

World Trade Organisation (WTO): replaced GATT in 1995 with a wider brief to regulate the world trading environment, reduce *tariff* barriers and help to resolve international trade disputes.

▓ The WTO has been reasonably successful in reducing *trade barriers* on manufactured goods but has been much less successful at dealing with the trade restraints surrounding agricultural products.

WTO: see *World Trade Organisation*.

x-inefficiency: when a *firm's* average cost curve is not at its lowest attainable level.
- It results from a lack of competition that has given rise to inefficiencies in the coordination and control of work practices. If a large firm has a significant level of *monopoly power* in either the private or public sector of the economy, management and workers may become careless in their attitude towards minimising unit costs.

yield: see *dividend yield*.

yield curve: a line that represents the relationship between the *rate of return* on bonds and their date of maturity.
- The curve is usually upward sloping from left to right as people will require a higher reward for parting with liquidity over longer periods of time. However, it can become inverted if there is a strong expectation that interest rates will fall in the future.

y-inefficiency: occurs when a firm with significant market power and little competition has become lax about the market opportunities that exist and has not recognised the potential for new customers, or the fact that a different market price might increase profits.
- There are similarities with x-efficiency in that they are both based on a level of incompetence and can occur in the private or public sector of the economy. However, it could be possible for a firm to be only x or y inefficient as one deals in costs and the other in potential revenues.

zero-rated: Customs and Excise rate certain products for *value added tax* at zero and the producer can claim back the VAT paid on inputs.
- This is different from products which are exempt from VAT, as tax already paid on inputs cannot be claimed back.
- *e.g.* Zero-rated products include food and books, while education and health are exempt products.

zero-sum game: in *game theory* it is where the gains by one player can only be at the expense of the other player.
- *e.g.* If the total size of a mature market is fixed, then the only way that one firm can increase its market share is to take orders away from other firms.

The most essential terms for the AQA, Edexcel and OCR 2000+ specifications

AQA

AS Module 1 *Markets and Market Failure*

allocative mechanism
complementary products and
    substitutes
demand and supply curves
derived demand
economic problem
elasticity: demand, supply, income,
    equilibrium price and output
factors of production
firm

industry
market
movements and shifts
opportunity cost
positive economics and normative
    economics
production possibility curve
profit
scarcity
trade-off

AS Module 2 *The National Economy*

aggregate demand and aggregate supply
balance of payments
Common Agricultural Policy
demerit good and merit good
distribution of income and distribution
    of wealth
economic efficiency
economic growth
economic welfare and social welfare
economies of scale
European Union
externality

fiscal policy and monetary policy
full employment
index number
inflation
market
market failure and market imperfection
monopoly
national income, real and nominal
public good
supply side economics
transport economics
unemployment

AS Module 3 *Markets at Work*

cost–benefit analysis
economic growth
elasticity of supply/demand
exchange rate
externality
firm
income elasticity of demand
indirect tax
industry

interest rate
market
monopoly
mortgage
neighbourhood effect
pollution rights
private property rights
supply side economics

A2 Module 4 *Working as an Economist*

This paper is examined as either a case study or coursework and the essential words will depend upon the chosen topic. If the case study is chosen, then for 2002/3/4 the topic is European Union.

Common Agricultural Policy
common external tariff
customs union
economic development
economic growth
euro
European Central Bank
hypothesise
inflation and unemployment
interest rate

Maastricht Treaty
monetary policy
monopoly power
regional policy
Single European Act
single European currency
trade barrier
trade creation and trade diversion
transparency
transport economics

A2 Module 5 *Business Economics and the Distribution of Income*

barriers to entry
consumer surplus and producer
    surplus
contestable market
cost–benefit analysis
diminishing marginal returns
distribution of income, distribution of
    wealth
economic efficiency
economies of scale and diseconomies
    of scale
fixed costs and variable costs
government failure

horizontal integration and vertical
    integration
marginal revenue product curve
monopolies, mergers and restrictive
    practices acts
monopoly and perfect competition
monopsony
oligopoly and kinked demand curve
price discrimination
profit and profit maximising rule
sales maximisation hypothesis
satisficing behaviour
short run and long run

A2 Module 6 *Government Policy, the National and International Economy*

balance of payments
comparative advantage
economic growth
euro
exchange rate
fiscal policy and monetary policy
globalisation
inflation and unemployment
liquidity preference theory
monetarism

Monetary Policy Committee
NAIRU
national income
Phillips curve
quantity theory of money
single European currency
standard of living
supply side economics
trade barrier

Edexcel

AS Unit 1 *Markets — How They Work*

buffer stock ✓

comparative advantage ✓

consumer surplus and producer ✓
   surplus

cross-price elasticity of demand ✓

economies of scale ✓

equilibrium price and output ✓

exchange rate ✓

incidence of taxation ✓

income elasticity of demand ✓

indirect tax ✓

labour market ✓

market ✓

national minimum wage ✓

normative economics and positive ✓
   economics

opportunity cost and scarcity ✓

price elasticity of demand and price ✓
   elasticity of supply

production possibility curve ✓

specialisation of function and division ✓
   of labour

subsidy ✓

supply curve and demand curve ✓

AS Unit 2 *Markets — Why They Fail*

barriers to entry ✓

congestion cost ✓

demerit good and merit good ✓

economic efficiency

economic welfare

economies of scale ✓

externality ✓

government failure ✓

market failure and market imperfection ✓

monopoly ✓

monopoly, merger and restrictive
   practices acts

neighbourhood effect

non-excludability ✓

non-rival product ✓

Pareto optimum

pollution ✓

pollution rights

private property rights ✓

public good ✓

AS Unit 3 *Managing the Economy*

aggregate demand ✓

aggregate supply ✓

balance of payments ✓

budget and fiscal policy ✓

distribution of income and distribution ✓
   of wealth

economic growth ✓

exchange rate ✓

full employment and under-full ✓
   employment equilibrium

gross domestic product ✓

gross national product ✓

inflation ✓

monetary policy ✓

Monetary Policy Committee ✓

multiplier

nominal and real ✓

Pareto optimum ✓

Phillips curve ✓

production possibility curve ✓

retail price index ✓

supply side economics ✓

unemployment ✓

A2 Unit 4 *Industrial Economics*

barriers to entry
concentration ratio
consumer surplus and producer surplus
contestable market
cost–plus pricing
economic efficiency
horizontal integration and vertical
   integration
markets
monopolies, mergers and restrictive
   practices acts

monopolistic competition
monopoly
monopoly power
multinational corporation
oligopoly
perfect competition
price discrimination
profit-maximising rule
sales maximisation hypothesis
satisficing behaviour
utility regulator

A2 Unit 5a *Labour Markets*

backward bending supply curve of labour
demand curve for labour and
   supply curve for labour
dependency ratio
distribution of income and distribution
   of wealth
Equal Pay Act
labour market
labour mobility
leisure and work
Lorenz curve

marginal rate of tax
marginal revenue product curve
monopsony
national minimum wage
poverty trap
regional policy
Social Charter
trade union
unemployment
wage differential
welfare state

A2 Unit 5b *Economic Development*

capital
comparative advantage
dependency ratio
economic development and economic
   growth
export-led growth and import
   substitution
globalisation
Harrod–Domar growth model
human capital

human development index
IBRD
IMF
less developed country
newly industrialising country
pollution
poverty
sustainability
technical progress
World Trade Organisation

A2 Unit 6 *The UK in the Global Economy*

augmented Phillips curve
balance of payments
Common Agricultural Policy
demand management and supply
   side economics
deregulation
direct tax and indirect tax
European Union
fiscal policy
fixed exchange rate and floating
   exchange rate

globalisation
inflation and unemployment
monetary policy
multinational corporation
NAIRU
public sector borrowing requirement
single European currency
tariff and quota
trade barrier
trade liberalisation
World Trade Organisation

OCR

AS Module 2881 *The Market System*

average cost and average revenue
barriers to entry
consumer surplus and producer
  surplus
demand curve and supply curve
division of labour and specialisation
  of function
economies of scale
elasticity of demand and elasticity
  of supply
equilibrium price and output
factors of production

long run and short run
marginal cost and marginal revenue
market
money
monopolistic competition
monopoly
movements and shifts
oligopoly
opportunity cost
perfect competition
production possibility curve
profit-maximising rule

AS Module 2882 *Market Failure and Government Intervention*

cost–benefit analysis
economic efficiency
excludable
externalities
firm
government
government failure
indirect tax
industry
labour mobility
market failure

market imperfection
merit good and demerit good
natural monopoly
non-excludability
Pareto optimum
production possibility curve
public good
rival and non-rival product
subsidy
supply side economics
utility regulator

AS Module 2883 *The National and International Economy*

aggregate demand and aggregate
  supply
balance of payments
economic growth
European Union
exchange rate
exports and imports
fiscal policy
full employment
government expenditure and
  taxation

gross domestic product
gross national product
inflation
injection and withdrawal
investment and saving
monetary policy
nominal and real
supply side economics
sustainability
trade barrier
unemployment

A2 Module 2884 *Economics of Work and Leisure*

backward bending supply curve
   of labour
collective bargaining and trade union
contestable market
demand curve for labour and supply
   curve for labour
economic efficiency
economic rent and transfer earnings
human capital
leisure and work
market failure

minimum wage legislation
monopolistic competition
monopoly
non-pecuniary benefit
oligopoly
perfect competition
poverty trap
profit-maximising rule
Social Charter
unit labour cost
wage

A2 Module 2885 *Transport Economics*

contestable market
cost–benefit analysis
denationalisation
deregulation
derived demand
externality
fixed costs and variable cost
   of production
franchising
integrated transport policy

investment
load factor
market failure and market
   imperfection
public good
road pricing
social optimum
sustainability
track costs
transport modes

A2 Module 2886 *Economics of Development*

absolute advantage and comparative
   advantage
dependency ratio
economic development and
   economic growth
exchange rate
export-led growth
Harrod–Domar growth model
human development index
import substitution
less developed country
national income

newly industrialising country
poverty
primary, secondary, tertiary,
   quaternary industry
Rostow's growth model
steady state growth
sustainability
trade liberalisation
unemployment
World Bank
World Trade Organisation

A2 Module 2887 *The UK Economy*

absolute advantage and comparative
  advantage
budget
direct tax and indirect tax
economic welfare
exchange equalisation account
exchange rate
fiscal policy and monetary policy
globalisation
inflation, unemployment and
  Phillips curve
investment

liquidity preference theory
loanable funds theory
Lorenz curve
Marshall–Lerner condition
money supply
multiplier
national income
public sector borrowing
  requirement
quota and tariff
supply side economics
wealth

A2 Module 2888 *Economics in a European Context*

capitalism
centrally planned economy
Common Agricultural Policy
comparative advantage
cost–benefit analysis
customs union
economic efficiency
European Central Bank
externality
globalisation

gradualism
labour mobility
Maastricht Treaty
market failure
privatisation
Single European Act
single European currency
trade barrier
trade liberalisation
transitional economy